Fine WoodWorking

DESIGN BOOK FIVE

Fine WoodWorking®
DESIGN BOOK FIVE

259
photographs
of the best
work in
wood

With
an essay
by Scott Landis
on Northwest
woodworkers

The Taunton Press

FRONT-COVER PHOTOGRAPH:

BRETON FLANNERY WOODWORKS
Freeport, Maine

Southwestern-style reading chair
(see page 61)

BACK-COVER PHOTOGRAPHS:

STEVEN IRVIN
San Antonio, Tex.

Sideboard
(see page 15)

GREG RACZOK
Grand Rapids, Mich.

Small-item box
(see page 99)

RICHARD SCHNEIDER
Sequim, Wash.

"Jini" recording guitar
(see page 123)

...*by fellow enthusiasts*

©1990 by The Taunton Press, Inc.
All rights reserved

First printing: May 1990

A FINE WOODWORKING Book

FINE WOODWORKING® is a trademark of The Taunton Press, Inc.,
registered in the U.S. Patent and Trademark Office.

The Taunton Press
63 South Main Street
Box 5506
Newtown, Connecticut 06470-5506

Contents

"I made my things because they weren't there.
I knew that if I didn't make them they would never be here,
and I very much wanted them to be here."

—Emmett E. Day, Jr.
Seattle, Washington
1948-1989

Introduction

There's something special about woodworkers. Perhaps it's the discipline that comes from working an unpredictable, often recalcitrant material that never completely yields to the maker's will. Or maybe it's the humility of knowing that the wood itself is so naturally appealing that human attempts to fashion it into beautiful objects never seem to do justice to the material itself.

Perhaps it's an awareness that each of us is a small thread in a complex tapestry of craft that's been enriched by every culture for as long as there have been people. For as far back as you care to look, woodworking has embraced the primitive and the sophisticated, the functional and the artistic, the practical and the fanciful and everything in between. This book, I believe, proves that our contemporary culture carries on the tradition.

A few years ago, I began to worry that the vigorous woodworking revival of the mid-1970s was beginning to fade. After some 15 years, a seen-it-all attitude seemed inevitable. But the open invitation we issued to readers of *Fine Woodworking* magazine in early 1989 to send us photographs of their best work proved that my fears were unfounded. We received more than 1,600 entries totaling 10,000 photos—all for a book that had room for fewer than 300.

During the summer of 1989, the editors of *Fine Woodworking* convened to select the photos for *Design Book Five.* The task proved difficult. We found the work to be universally good and alive with the energy of makers—professional and amateur—presenting both new ideas and fresh interpretations of familiar themes. As judges, we often paused to study a piece to learn how the maker solved a particularly difficult construction challenge. The only bad thing about the competition was that it was too much of a good thing. There were enough good entries for several books, but we could print only one.

As editors and woodworkers, we travel regularly and visit with craftspeople in their shops and at galleries and shows. Our goal was to make a book that reflects our sense of what we've found to be the best in contemporary work. We looked for innovation in design and craftsmanship and sound construction practices. A good concept was essential but often, it was the little details like grain matching, molded edges or delicate inlay that made a great piece sparkle among a field of good pieces. We also tried to pick a representative sampling of styles, so that the book would reflect the true vitality of the craft, not just our tastes.

The judges frequently had to redefine their ideas. Do period reproductions have a place in a "design" book? Does a simple idea, executed exceptionally well but without ostentation and flourish, have a place here? Should we accept a piece solely on the grounds that the maker wanted to make best use of an exceptionally stunning piece of wood? How much glass, leather, metal, lacquer and paint should we allow? We hope that the photographs presented here give you a good idea of how we resolved these questions and that you enjoy our view of the state of our craft.

Lovely as they are, the photographs in this book represent the very tops of the trees, the veneer on the piece, the finish coat of varnish. Beyond what you see here are the lives of the craftspeople who've learned to work wood at the highest level. Who are they? How have they come to be woodworkers? How do they survive making enduring objects in a culture that values instant gratification and throwaway goods?

Last year we sent writer Scott Landis on a quest for answers to these questions. We chose one region—the Pacific Northwest—as a microcosm of the rest of the country. The Northwest has a fascinating mix of ancient Indian culture, a rebounding forest economy and a recent immigrant population of talented artisans. By concentrating on this region, we found craftspeople in contexts not unlike what you'd meet in other parts of the country. Landis' essay, Design in Context, begins on p. 146.

This book represents a great deal of work by a talented staff. I am grateful to the editors of *Fine Woodworking,* who took time from their demanding magazine duties to jury the photos. Special thanks go to the editorial assistants who processed the slides, but especially to Cassandra Lincoln, whose patient and accurate work kept each slide matched to its entry blank. Finally, I extend deep thanks to the readers who sent us their valuable photos, without which this book would not have been possible.

Dick Burrows
May, 1990

Cabinets

RICK NORRANDER
Portland, Ore.

Display cabinet
Honduras mahogany
30 in. x 22 in. x 72 in.
Photo by Brian Erickson

4

STEVEN HOLMAN
Dorset, Vt.

Corner cabinet
Oak, bubinga, maple, black
lacquer, rosewood
32 in. x 22 in. x 84 in.
Photo by Cook Neilson

MICHAEL C. FORTUNE
Toronto, Ontario, Canada

Etagère
Macassar ebony, anigre, glass
44 in. x 14 in. x 82 in.
Photo by D. Allen

DARRYL KEIL
Freeport, Maine

Credenza
Ebonized cherry, tineo veneer
68 in. x 18½ in. x 32 in.
Photo by Stretch Tuemmler

DANIEL PECK
San Antonio, Tex.

Corner cabinet
American white oak, English
brown oak, walnut, granite
26½ in. x 84 in.
Photo by Swain Edens Studio

LANCE PATTERSON
Boston, Mass.

Blanket chest
Quartered red oak, rosewood
knobs, cedar
44 in. x 19 in. x 31 in.
Photo by Lance Patterson

RODGER REID
New Preston, Conn.

Corner cabinet
Mahogany
37 in. x 85 in.
Photo by William Seitz

JOHN P. McCORMACK
Cambridge, Mass.

Bombé chest
Mahogany, crotch mahogany
veneer, poplar
40½ in. x 20½ in. x 34⅝ in.
Photo by Lance Patterson

7

JOSEPH SCHWARTE
Evanston, Ill.

P-38 dresser #1
Cherry, maple, aromatic cedar,
steel
30 in. x 20 in. x 50 in.
Photo by Kim Larsen

WILLIAM BIVONA
Slocum, R. I.

Stereo cabinet
Cherry, walnut inlay
18 in. x 24 in. x 50 in.
Photo by Scott Smith

ROD WALES
Muddles Green, E. Sussex,
England

Shotgun cabinet
Fumed and white waxed oak,
maple, stainless steel
48 in. x 23 in. x 50 in.
Photo by M. Hemsley

W. S. HOWARD
Boston, Mass.

TV cabinet
Ash, ebony
66 in. x 24 in. x 30 in.
Photo by Lance Patterson

CHARLES SWANSON
Providence, R. I.

"I have a leg to stand on"
Masonite, curly maple, bronze
44 in. x 15 in. x 42 in.
Photo by Charles Swanson

COLIN REID
Oakland, Calif.

Sideboard
Wenge, curly maple
88 in. x 20 in. x 30 in.
Photo by John DeGroot

STEPHEN OUBRE
East Aurora, N. Y.

"Evidement"
Bubinga, wenge, cherry,
sterling-silver inlay
20 in. x 40 in. x 60 in.
Photo by Tony Gerardi

ROBERT J. VOVES
Sedona, Ariz.

Lingerie cabinet
Curly maple, maple, colored-
lacquer finish
28 in. x 24 in. x 72 in.
Photo by Michelle Breedlove

ROGER SHERRY
Staten Island, N. Y.

Rolling sideboard/bar
Bird's-eye maple, birch, marble
56 in. x 18 in. x 36 in.
Photo by John Kuatik

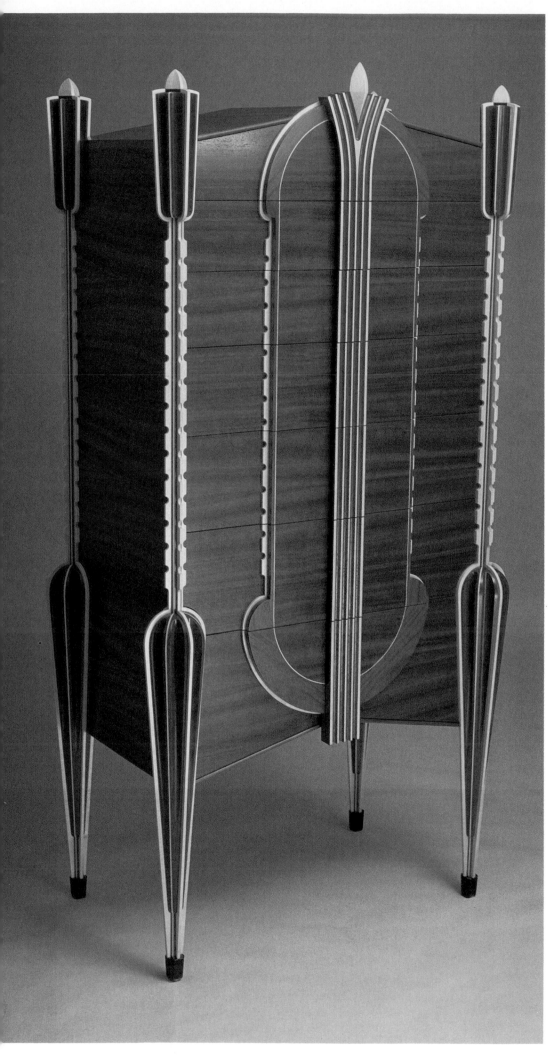

THOMAS J. BECK
Philadelphia, Pa.

Tall chest of drawers
Padauk, maple
36 in. x 24 in. x 72 in.
Photo by Thomas J. Beck

JON FROST
St. Paul, Minn.

Hi-fi cabinet
Quilted mahogany veneer,
Honduras mahogany, ebony
24 in. x 17 in. x 48 in.
Photo by Jim Gallop

BILL BRACE
Concord, Mass.

Music chest
Maple, padauk, ebony
26 in. x 20 in. x 56 in.
Photo by Dean Powell

ROGER HEITZMAN
Scotts Valley, Calif.

Credenza
Maple
65 in. x 22 in. x 32 in.
Photo by Roger Heitzman

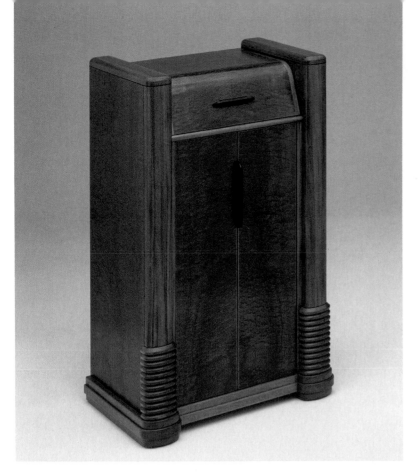

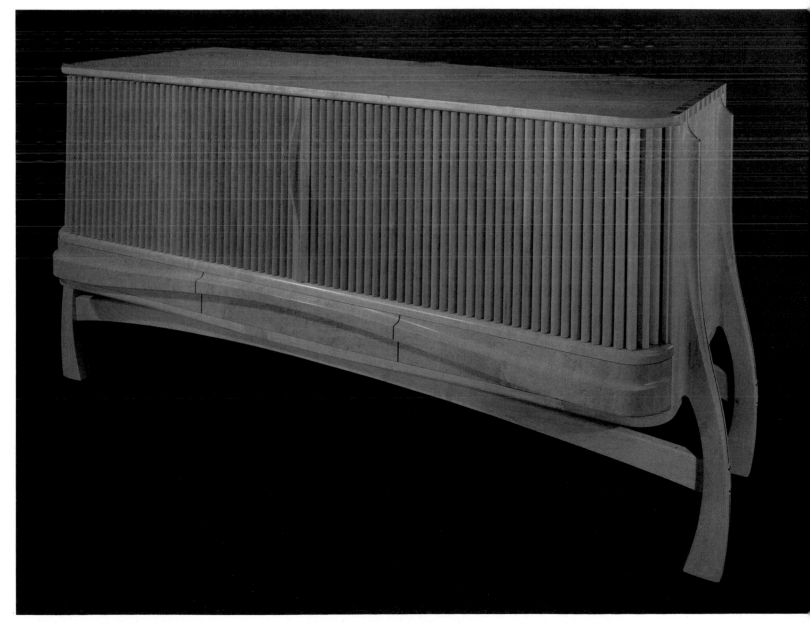

KARL NIELSEN
Oak Harbor, Wash.

Fluted liquor cabinet
Curly maple, ebony, brass
34 in. x 18 in. x 64 in.
Photo by Karl Nielsen

STEVEN IRVIN
San Antonio, Tex.

Sideboard
Wenge, sapele, ivory
70 in. x 19 in. x 34 in.
Photo by Swain Edens Studio

PETER NARAMORE
Kula, Hawaii

Nightstands
Mango, ebony
26 in. x 18 in. x 22 in.
Photo by Steve Minkowski

GEORGE GORDON
Reboboth, Mass.

Liquor/display cabinet
Walnut, walnut crotch veneer,
curly white ash
44 in. x 22 in. x 68 in.
Photo by Douglas Dalton

JON P. ALLEY
Churchville, Pa.

Wall-hung storage cabinet
Mahogany, maple plywood,
goncalo alves
20 in. x 8½ in. x 34 in.
Photo by David Graham

JEFFREY WASSERMAN
Norwood, Mass.

Chest of drawers
Tinted ash, ash plywood
50 in. x 20 in. x 48 in.
Photo by Dean Powell

THOMAS C. RICKE
Cincinnati, Ohio

Dresser unit
Bird's-eye maple, purpleheart
40 in. x 24 in. x 34 in.
Photo by Jon Keeling

WENDY MARUYAMA
Berkeley, Calif.

Credenza
Bleached Honduras mahogany
18 in. x 38 in. x 72 in.
Photo by Cary Okazaki

GEOFFREY WARNER
Exeter, R. I.

Television cabinet
Sapele, dyed curly maple,
wenge
48 in. x 24 in. x 82½ in.
Photo by Dean Powell

GERT BECKER
Redmond, Wash.

Baroque linen cabinet
Sugar pine, white oak
42 in. x 80 in.
Photo by Loyd Weller

BRAD SCHWARTZ
Deer Isle, Maine

Display cabinet
Pecan, bocote, cocobolo,
handmade glass
22 in. x 65 in.
Photo by David Klopenstein

ROBB YOUNG
Honolulu, Hawaii

Chest of drawers
Koa
100 in. x 22 in. x 44 in.
Photo by Kastner Design

DAVID SAVAGE
Bideford, Devon, England

Collector's cabinet
Macassar ebony, white English
holly, oak, cedar
18 in. x 12½ in. x 63 in.
Photo by John Gollop

PAULA GARBARINO
Somerville, Mass.

Cupboard
Cherry, poplar, holly
59 in. x 19 in. x 79 in.
Photo by Stephen Morse

JAMIE ROBERTSON
Cambridge, Mass.

Lunettes
Macassar ebony, holly,
harewood veneers, ebonized
walnut
24 in. x 15 in. x 26 in.
Photo by Dean Powell

SUSAN PFEIFFER
Elizabethtown, Ky.

"Trees and Falling"
Cherry, wenge, maple,
purpleheart, zebrawood
18 in. x 13 in. x 64 in.
Photo by Tom Eckert

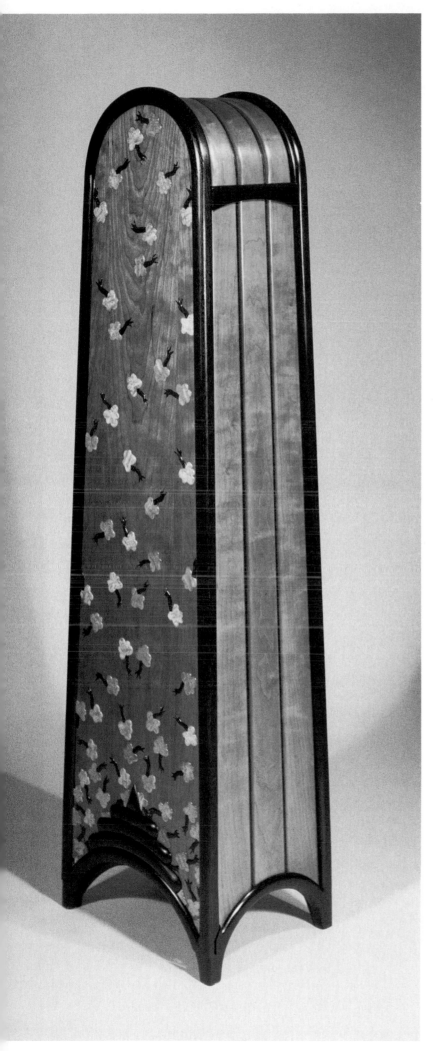

Desks

SCOTT RICHNER
Green Acres, Wash.

Detail: Fall-flap secretary
(see page 25)

ROBERT DIEMERT
Toronto, Ontario, Canada

Demi-lune cabinet
Pomele mahogany, East Indian
rosewood, purpleheart, maple
54 in. x 18 in. x 30 in.
Photo by John O'Brien

ALAN WILKINSON
Wahiawa, Hawaii

Rolltop desk
Koa, curly koa, rosewood, ebony
64 in. x 30 in. x 46 in.

SCOTT RICHNER
Green Acres, Wash.

Secretary
Honduras mahogany, crab apple,
Brazilian rosewood, leather
27 in. x 16 in. x 48 in.
Photo by Robert Barros

GLEN G. GRANT
Andover, Mass.

Bombé slant-top desk with
serpentine front
South American mahogany,
poplar
32 in. x 18 in. x 40 in.
Photo by Spectrum
Photography

RICHARD P. ETRE
Shrewsbury, Mass.

Federal tambour desk
Mahogany, mahogany crotch
veneer, satinwood
40 in. x 40 in. x 42 in.
Photo by Susan DeLong

ROBERT W. HOEL
N. Quincy, Mass.

"The Musical Maple Walnut
Unicorn Desk"
Maple, walnut
70 in. x 24 in. x 75 in.
Photo by Wendell A. Davis, Jr.

ANDREW JACOBSON
Petaluma, Calif.

Writing desk
Quilted cherry, rosewood
54 in. x 26 in. x 29¾ in.
Photo by Dennis Anderson

JEREMIAH E. de RHAM
Boston, Mass.

Writing desk
Cherry, rosewood, soft maple
57½ in. x 33½ in. x 37 in.
Photo by Jeremiah E. de Rham

RICHARD FORD, JR.
New Bedford, Mass.

Desk
Curly maple, maple burl, bubinga
51 in. x 22 in. x 30 in.
Photo by Dean Powell

JIM PAYNE
Santa Cruz, Calif.

Writing desk and chair
Sugar pine
40 in. x 24 in. x 50 in.
Photo by Paul Schraub

KEN SCHOEN
Middlebury, Vt.

Desk
Cherry, maple
60 in. x 32 in. x 30 in.
Photo by Erik Borg

JOHN MARCOUX
Providence, R. I.

Precis desk
Basswood, stainless steel;
sandblasted, painted steel
46 in. x 22 in. x 28 in.
Photo by Dean Powell

JOHN CLARK
Easthampton, Mass.

"Good government/good citizens"
ColorCore®, hotworked glass (by
Ken Carder), curly oak
60 in. x 26 in. x 54 in.
Photo by Michael Latil

STEVEN ROUETTE
Chino Valley, Ariz.

Desk and chair
Native Arizona oak, gambel
41 in. x 22 in. x 31 in.
Photo by David Schmidt

31

JAMES SAGUI
Boston, Mass.

Writing desk/side table
East Indian rosewood, curly
maple
Photo by Dean Powell

TERRY MOORE
Newport, N. H.

Fall-front secretaire
Mahogany, Brazilian rosewood
36 in. x 14 in. x 48 in.
Photo by Thomas Ames

T. EVAN HUGHES
Washington, D. C.

Rolltop desk
Walnut, ebony, leather
42 in. x 28 in. x 38 in.
Photo by Edward Owen

DAN MOSHEIM
Arlington, Vt.

Desk
Mahogany
42 in. x 30 in. x 42 in.
Photo by Cook Neilson

DAVID B BARTH
Brooklyn, N. Y.

Jewelry/silver chest and table
Lacewood, walnut
24 in. x 12 in. x 30 in.
Photo by John Anderson

DAVID ORTH
Oak Park, Ill.

"Atlantis table"
Maple, lacquer, glass
42 in. x 42 in. x 32 in.
Photo by Al Derre

PHILLIP R. TENNANT
Indianapolis, Ind.

Sofa table
Maple, granite, brass, glass
60 in. x 18 in. x 28 in.
Photo by Patrick Bennett

DIERK STANGE
Hamburg, Germany

Table with removable leaf
Mahogany, East Indian
palisander, maple
67 in. x 43 in. x 30 in.
Photo by Uli Muller

STEPHEN TURINO
Charlestown, R. I.

End tables
Macassar ebony, curly maple
20 in. x 15 in. x 22 in.
Photo by Dean Powell

ROBERT B. MATERNE
Bristol, R. I.

Hall table
Mahogany, fiddleback
mahogany, ebony, holly
48 in. x 18 in. x 30 in.
Photo by Martin Doyle

GEORGE LEVIN
Seattle, Wash.

Dressing table and stool
Walnut, elm, yellow cedar
45 in. x 19 in. x 27 in.
Photo by Robert Milne

39

GEORGE KUIPERS
Toronto, Ontario, Canada

Coffee table
White ash, glass
48 in. x 48 in. x 18 in.
Photo by C. Lantinga

GLEN GURNER
Boston, Mass.

"Halo table #1"
Birch plywood, apple plywood,
poplar, polychromed with
zolatone
24-in. dia. x 30 in.
Photo by Charles Mayer

EDWARD ZUCCA
Woodstock, Conn.

Dining table
Curly maple, mahogany, ebony
78 in. x 42 in. x 30 in.
Photo by Edward Zucca

GEORGE REZENDES
San Francisco, Calif.

Dining table
Cherry, ebonized ash
52-in. dia. x 29 in.

41

PETER A. CHRISMAN
Tuscon, Ariz.

End tables
Mesquite
20 in. x 18 in. x 22 in.
Photo by Victor LaViola

RON DIEFENBACHER
St. Louis, Mo.

Seltzer table
Cherry, ebony
72 in. x 42 in. x 29 in.
Photo by Randall Hyman

TODD OUWEHAND
Los Angeles, Calif.

Arched table
Walnut, ebony
12 in. x 12 in. x 16 in.
Photo by Mark Adams

MARK DALE SMITH and RENE HILL
New Meadows, Idaho

Peccary and prickly pear console
Walnut, cherry, pine
60 in. x 28 in. x 28 in.
Photo by Steve Welsh

43

LLOYD PARCELL
Unionville, Va.

Tea table
Honduras mahogany
30 in. x 18 in. x 26 in.
Photo by John DeVivi

W. MICKEY CALLAHAN
Cambridge, Mass.

Federal work table
Mahogany, ebony, satinwood, East
Indian rosewood, holly
20½ in. x 16½ in. x 28 in.
Photo by Lance Patterson

FOSTER CORTIS
Avalon Beach, New South
Wales, Australia

"Dragon table"
Brazilian mahogany, Queensland
white beech, gold
18½ in. x 20½ in. x 15 in.
Photo by Mike Simmons

DALE LEWIS
Birmingham, Ala.

"Dem Dry Bones"
Wenge, cherry
22½ in. x 19½ in. x 31½ in.
Photo by Dale Lewis

LEE F. KARKRUFF
Pompey, N. Y.

Dressing table and chair
Curly purpleheart veneer, curly
and quilted maple
52 in. x 20 in. x 59½ in.
Photo by William Gandino

BRUCE ASBIL
Mississauga, Ontario, Canada

Coffee table
White ash
29 in. x 29 in. x 15 in.
Photo by Bruce Asbil

HEARTWOOD CRAFTSMEN, Inc.
Philadelphia, Pa.

Conference table
African mahogany, ebony, hand-
rubbed lacquer
30 in. x 16-ft. dia.
Photo by Gary McKinnis

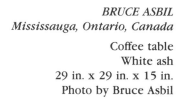

STEVEN D. SOVELOVE
Point Reyes Station, Calif.

Coffee table
Cherry
46 in. x 20 in. x 17 in.
Photo by Steven D. Sovelove

MARK SFIRRI and ROBERT DODGE
New Hope, Pa.

Hall table
Wenge, vermilion, Corian®, acrylic, gold leaf
40 in. x 18 in. x 34 in.
Photo by David Graham

CRAIG NUTT
Northport, Ala.

Carrot table
16-in. dia. x 26 in.
Photo by Rickey Yanaura

RICHARD CHALMERS
Mattapoisett, Mass.

Hall table
Walnut, brass, lacquer
42 in. x 12 in. x 34 in.
Photo by Roger Birn

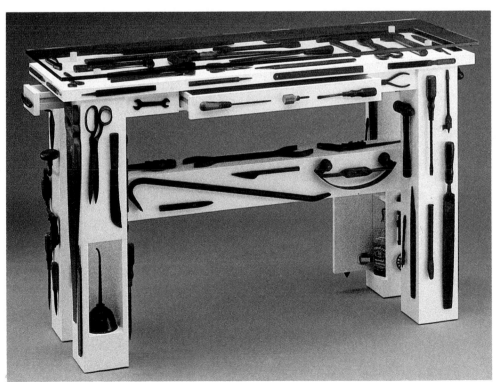

A. LAMAR SMITH
Birmingham, Ala.

"Grandfather table"
Birch plywood, alder
60 in. x 20 in. x 39½ in.
Photo by Ralph Anderson

Chairs

TURNER BROOKS and KEN SCHOEN
Middlebury, Vt.

Adirondack-inspired chair
Mahogany, plywood
30 in. x 26 in. x 46 in.
Photo by Erik Borg

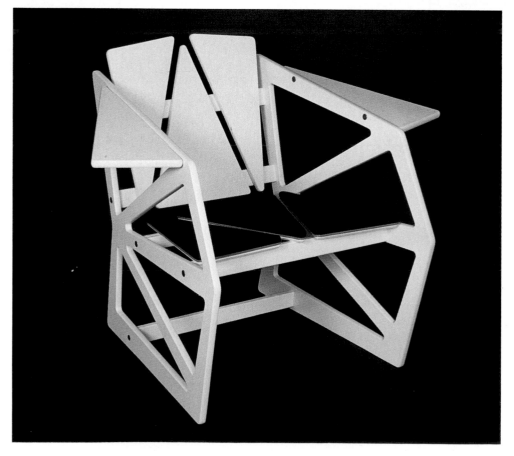

JOHN McALEVEY
Warner, N. H.

Settee chest
Ebonized mahogany
48 in. x 22 in. x 36 in.
Photo by Timothy Savard

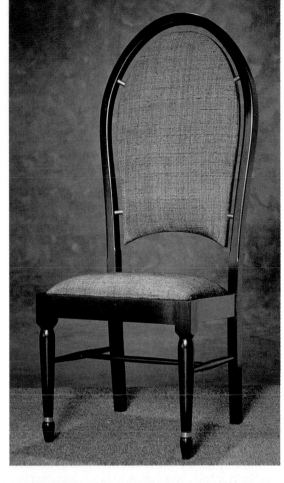

MICHAEL STERLING
Chico, Calif.

Fillaric chair
Claro walnut, white oak, Baltic
birch plywood, brass, silk
17½ in. x 19¾ in. x 52 in.
Photo by Mike Agliolo

HELGE OLSEN and BOB
MORGAN
Davis, Calif.

Knock-down chair
Baltic birch plywood, wool
27½ in. x 40 in. x 33 in.
Photo by Barbara Molloy

JOSEPH J. BRIEN
West Cornwall, Conn.

Side chair
Baltic birch plywood, maple
and ash dowels, black lacquer
19 in. x 20 in. x 32 in.
Photo by Joseph Brien

CLAY FREEMAN
Dallas, Tex.

Fireside chair
Maple, birch, leather
33 in. x 25 in. x 33 in.
Photo by Brian Harness

ROB OGILVIE
Nashville, Tenn.

Side chair
Birch
19 in. x 19 in. x 54 in.
Photo by Alan Messer

IRA A. KEER and BRUCE KIEFFER
Minneapolis, Minn.

"Daphy: A Winged Armchair"
Bird's-eye maple, curly maple,
ebonized walnut, mahogany
32 in. x 43½ in. x 41½ in.
Photo by Steve Greenway

GARY PATTENDEN
Brockville, Ontario, Canada

Wishbone chair
Cherry, leather
30 in. x 28 in. x 35 in.

PETER REILLY
Providence, R. I.

Dining chairs
Cherry, impact leather
18 in. x 37 in.
Photo by Roger Birn

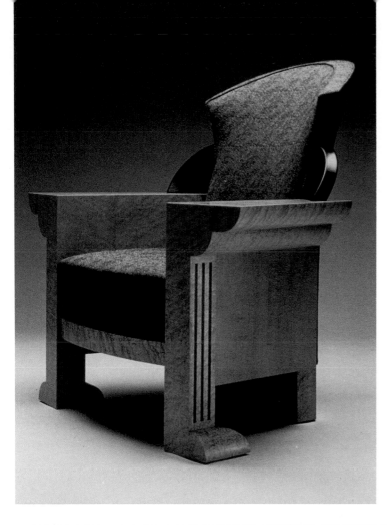

ALEXANDER B. KRUTSKY
Boston, Mass.

Chippendale side chair
Walnut
23 in. x 40 in.x 20 in.
Photo by Lance Patterson

KEN MORAN
Portland, Ore.

Dining chair
Cherry, silk
18 in. x 18 in. x 52 in.
Photo by Jim Piper

EDWIN B. TEALE
Aloha, Ore.

Ribbon-back Chippendale chair
Walnut
27 in. x 18 in. x 38½ in.
Photo by Keith Aden

BRUCE PETERSON
Taos, N. Mex.

Saarinen chairs
Cherry, mahogany, lacquer, silk
18 in. x 19 in. x 38 in.
Photo by Douglas Kahn

GREGG LIPTON
Portland, Maine

Circle-back chairs
Pickled ash, purpleheart
18 in. x 18 in. x 36 in.
Photo by John Tanabe

RICHARD A. ZAYATZ
Arvada, Colo.

Plus Vite #1
Maple, poplar, plywood
35 in. x 24¼ in. x 36½ in.
Photo by Dan Sidor

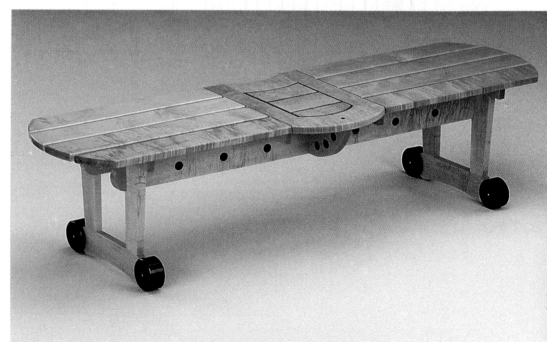

MARK NATHENSON
Rochester, N. Y.

Bench
Maple, ebonized maple,
mother of pearl
70 in. x 22 in. x 17 in.
Photo by Hampton Bridwell

DANIEL ABRAMSON
Dover, N. H.

Modern interpretation of Italian
Renaissance folding chair
White oak
16½ in. x 36 in.x 18 in.
Photo by Brian Gulick

*BRETON FLANNERY
WOODWORKS*
Freeport, Maine

Southwestern-style reading chair
Bleached ash
22 in. x 20 in. x 41 in.
Photo by John Tanabe

RUSS BUCKLEY
Rangiora, New Zealand

Bench seat
Philippine mahogany, cedar
63 in. x. 31 in. x 41 in.
Photo by Gary Senior

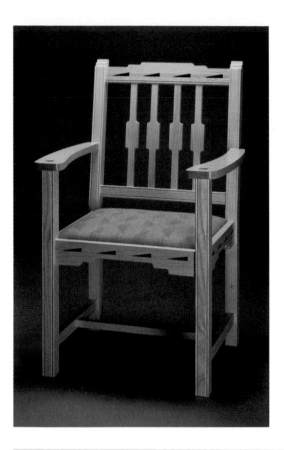

DALE BROHOLM
Jamaica Plain, Mass.

Couch
Bird's-eye maple (veneer and
solid), plywood, ash
72 in. x 28 in. x 36 in.
Photo by David DuBusc

JIM FAWCETT
Highland, N. Y.

"Delicate Romantic Balance"
Painted hardwood
35¾ in. x 21½ in. x 25½ in.
Photo by Will Faller

JAY McDOUGALL
Fergus Falls, Minn.

Window seat
Cherry, walnut
35 in. x 19 in. x 24 in.
Photo by Erik Saulitis

SCOTT AUBERGER
Churchville, N. Y.

Pair of side chairs
Ammonia-fumed red oak
18 in. x 18 in. x 45 in.
Photo by Scott Auberger

LARRY LAWLOR
Gualala, Calif.

Rocker and ottoman
Maple, ebony; handwoven
upholstery by Harriet Lichtenstein
45 in. x 24 in. x 44 in.
Photo by George Post

JAMES DOWLE
Kaikoura, New Zealand

Dining/desk chair
European ash
17 in x. 18 in. x 36 in.
Photo by Lloyd Park

DAVID W. SCOTT
Clyde, N. C.

Bench
Ash, blue-dyed veneer
48 in. x 18 in. x 28 in.
Photo by Steve Kuell

Beds

NICK HETZER
Cincinnati, Ohio

Youth bed
Teak
55 in. x 31 in. x 33 in.
Photo by Perry Wolfe

LAURA J. DYKZEUL
Seattle, Wash.

Queen-size bed
Bubinga, East Indian rosewood,
Gaboon ebony
80 in. x 62 in. x 32 in.
Photo by Gregg Krogstad

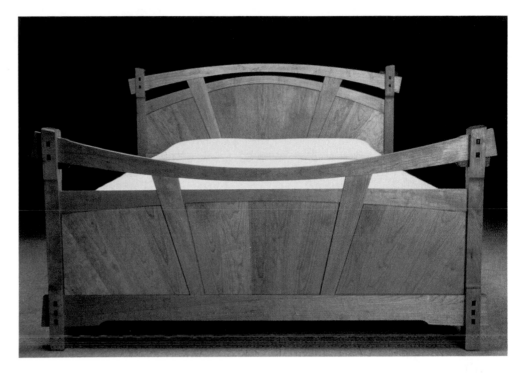

CHRISTOPHER WRIGHT
San Francisco Calif.

Queen-size bed
Cherry, wenge
88 in. x 68 in. x 47 in.
Photo by Todd Park

DAVID MAHAFFEY
Napa, Calif.

Laurel's crib
Walnut, madrone, rosewood
48 in. x 30 in. x 39 ½ in.
Photo by David Mahaffey

LOUIS J. NASSRAWAY
Lomita, Calif.

Cradle
Walnut, ebony
45 in. x 24 in. x 47 in.
Photo by Richard Karl Koch

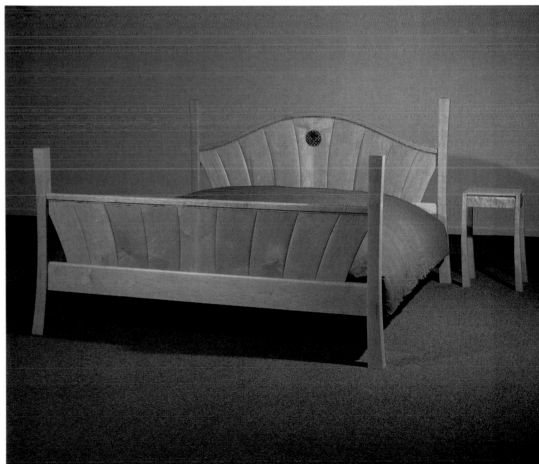

PAUL CARON
Asheville, N. C.

"Tiara" king-size bed
Maple, padauk
85 in. x 82 in. x 54 in.
Photo by J. Weiland

MARK ERICKSON
Oakland, Calif.

"Sweet Dreams"
Jelutong, basswood
82 in. x 48 in. x 72 in.
Photo by Mark Erickson

THOM ROSS
Portland, Ore.

Maple, maple veneer, dyes, brass
90 in. x 67 in. x 70 in.
Photo by Miriam Seger

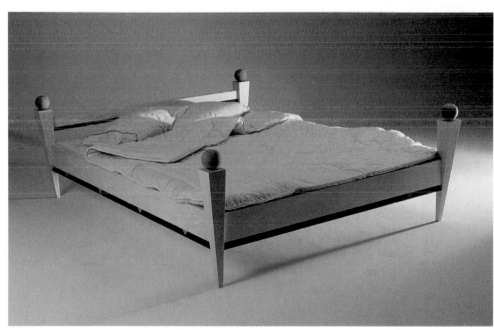

DAVID DOCHOW
Portland, Ore.

Vertigo bed
Ash, fir
88 in. x 66 in. x 28 in.
Photo by Miriam Seger

FRANK KLAUSZ and MICHAEL
KNEPP
Pluckemin, N. J.

Bedroom set
Purpleheart, ebony, ash
103 in. x 105 in.
Photos by Michael Moran

STAN JACOBS
San Diego, Calif.

"Silverleaf" queen-size bed
Riftsawn white oak
84 in. x 64 in. x 42 in.
Photo by Med Beuregard

R. THOMAS TEDROWE, JR.
Chicago Ill.

Bedroom set (queen-size bed)
Curly maple, Macassar ebony,
ebonized walnut
87 in. x 68 in. x 45 in..
Photo by R. Thomas Tedrowe, Jr.

RONALD PUCKETT
Richmond, Va.

Post and ball bed
Walnut, wenge
86 in. x 66 in. x 79 in.
Photo by Richard Larimer

LORNA SECREST and JEROME
JOSEPH
Pittsburgh, Pa.

Bed and end tables
Maple, pearwood, bloodwood
76 in. x 80 in. x 40 in.
Photo by Jerome Joseph

Bowls

DAN KVITKA
Corvallis, Ore.

"Banded Barrel"
Primavera
16 in. x 14-in. dia.
Photo by Dan Kvitka

BRUCE BERNSON
Santa Barbara, Calif.

"Spirit vessel"
Buckeye burl, ebony
8¼ in. x 8¼ in.
Photo by Mehosh Dziadzio

BOB KOPEC
Longwood, Fla.

Xylopot series #89-2
Walnut, zebrano, maple
7 in. x 9-in. dia.
Photo by Bob Kopec

DENNIS STEWART
Hillsboro, Ore.

Hollow vessel with three lips
Central American lignum vitae
(sandblasted)
7-in. dia.
Photo by Dennis Stewart

79

STEVE GELLMAN
Arcata, Calif.

Turned containers
Ebony, Brazilian rosewood,
holly
1⅞ in. x 1½-in. dia.
Photo by Pat Cudahy Studios

BARRY T. MacDONALD
Grosse Pointe Park, Mich.

"Carnival Canister"
Padauk, ebony, holly
7½ in. x 8½ in.
Photo by G. C. Moon

KIP CHRISTENSEN
Provo, Utah

Lidded container
Cocobolo, ebony, spalted maple
2¼ in. x 3¾-in. dia.
Photo by Glenn Anderson

R. W. CHATELAIN
Huntington, Vt.

Pair of contrasting wood bowls
Ebony, bloodwood, sterling
silver
3 in. x 5-in. dia.
Photo by Tommy Elder

JON N. SAUER
Daly City, Calif.

Containers
Blackwood, bamboo, lignum vitae,
kingwood, pink ivory
4 in. x 2-in. dia.
Photo by Richard Sargent

LINCOLN SEITZMAN
West Long Branch, N. J.

"Petrified Basket III"
Ash, afrormosia, ipé
17 in. x 13-in. dia.
Photo by Jeff Martin

PETER M. PETROCHKO
Oxford, Conn.

"Tent Structure Vessel"
Curly maple, ziricote, sugar maple
15½ in. x 15½-in. dia.
Photo by Frank Poole

FLETCHER COX
Tougaloo, Miss.

"Vegetable Soup Plate"
Wenge, maple, purpleheart
2 in. x 14 in. dia.
Photo by Fletcher Cox

MAX KRIMMEL
Boulder, Colo.

Vessel #107
Mahogany, vermilion, maple
4 in. x 24-in. dia.
Photo by Max Krimmel

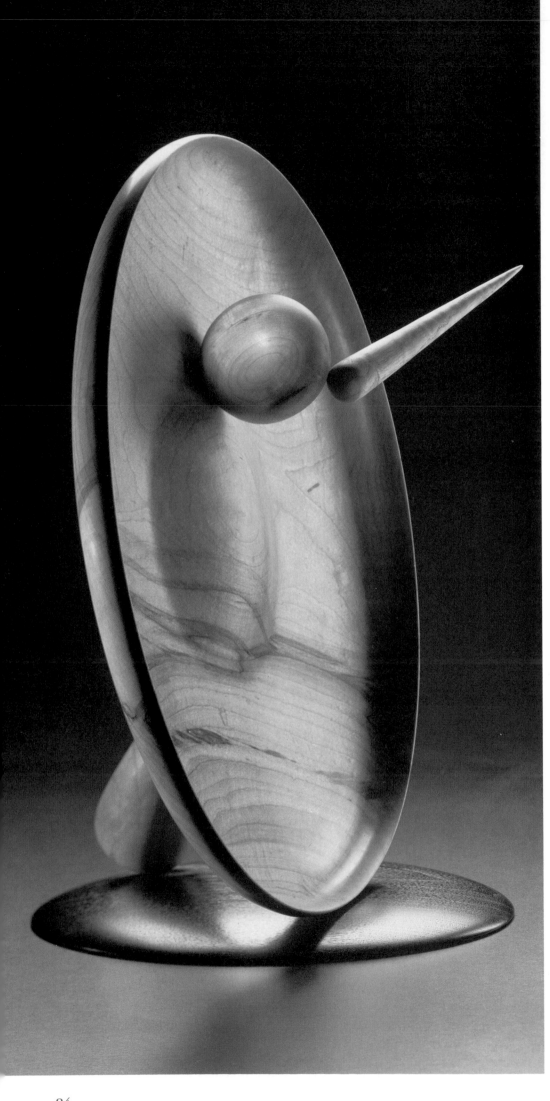

NEIL J. DONOVAN
Erie, Pa.

"Tangential Superfriction"
Soft maple, ash, cherry,
ebonized butternut
17-in. dia.
Photo by Mark Fainstein

PAUL RUHLMANN
Concord, Mass.

"Walnut/walnut: a container for
dreams and precious objects"
Walnut, bird's-eye maple, maple
13 in. x 11 in. x 18 in.
Photo by Paul Ruhlmann

JAMES STEPHENSON
Tempe, Ariz.

Segmented bowl
Curly maple, walnut, ebony
4¼ in. x 6-in. dia.
Photo by Jeff Scovil

TED HODGETTS
Millbrook, Ontario, Canada

Turned hollow vessel
Wenge, holly, ebony
9 in. x 8-in. dia.
Photo by Peter Hogan

RICHARD SULLIVAN
Corvallis, Ore.

"Ritual Vessel Form"
Black walnut
11 in. x 20-in. dia.
Photo by Dan Kvitka

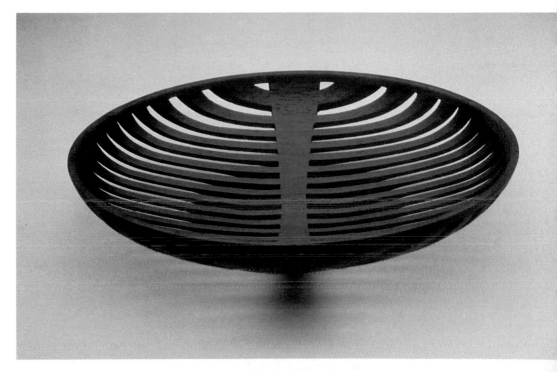

DEWEY N. GARRETT
Livermore, Calif.

Lattice vessel
Padauk
2 in. x 10-in. dia.
Photo by Creative Camera

MICHAEL HOSALUK
Saskatoon, Saskatchewan,
Canada

"Ancient Ruin"
Burnt elm
5 in. x 12-in. dia.
Photo by Grant Kernan

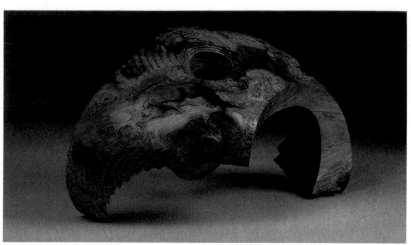

ROBERT SONDAY
Free Union, Va.

Bowl
Jarrah
5 in. x 6-in. dia.
Photo by D'Wayne Blackdog

STONEY LAMAR
Saluda, N. C.

"Seventh Sphere"
Cherry burl
17 in. x 7 in. x 8 in.
Photo by Evan Bracken

ROBYN HORN
Little Rock, Ark.

Redwood-root burl
19 in. x 12 in.
Photo by Bill Parsons

ROD CRONKITE
Racine, Wis.

"Clouds Rest"
White ash burl
10 in. x 9½-in. dia.
Photo by Jon Bolton

DENNIS ELLIOTT
Sherman, Conn.

Hollow vessel
Maple burl
6 in. x 12½-in. dia.
Photo by Iona S. Elliott

MICHAEL PETERSON
West Edmonds, Wash.

"Coastal Basket"
Myrtle, kingwood, tulipwood,
cocobolo
8 in. x 17-in. dia.

RON FLEMING
Tulsa, Okla.

Snakewood bud
Snakewood
7 in. x 5-in. dia.
Photo by Ron Fleming

ALAN DIXON
Brixham, Devon, England

Bowl of fruit
Ash, tulipwood, blackwood, pink
ivorywood, rosewood, yew
Photo by J. Bosley

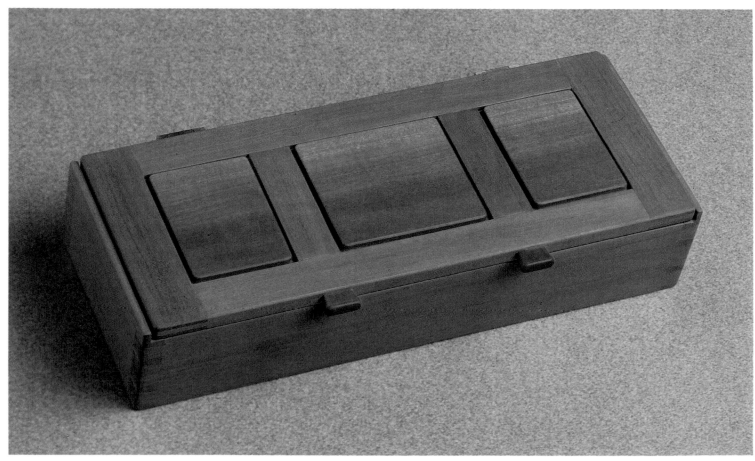

VICTOR CLAPP
Edmonton, Alberta, Canada

Fish box
Oak, walnut
12½ in. x 7 in. x 3½ in.
Photo by Ranson Photographers

JOHN L. HEATWOLE
Bridgewater, Va.

Election-Year Box
Linden
5½ in. x 3 in. x 1 in.
Photo by Dick McCrary

JOHN DUNHAM
Glens Falls, N. Y.

Blanket chest
Red oak, walnut, aromatic cedar
52 in. x 22 in. x 23 in.
Photo by Anthony Cosentino

KATHERINE HELLER
Pacific Grove, Calif.

Box
Pearwood, pink ivory
8¼ in. x 3¼ in. x 1¾ in.
Photo by Fred Stimson

TERRY L. EVANS
Olathe, Kan.

Kandinsky jewelry box
Narra, wenge, holly, ash,
persimmon, bubinga
10½ in. x 7 in. x 2 in.
Photo by Steve Attig

RICHARD MINOR
Springfield, Ore.

Toolbox
Quartersawn white oak,
American walnut
18 in. x 9 in. x 11 in.

ROBERT THEISS
Deadwood, Ore.

Blanket chest
Cherry
56 in. x 21¾ in. 22 in.
Photo by Kent Petterson

STEVE BRACKEN
Bozeman, Mont.

Jewelry box
Cherry, quilted maple
17¾ in. x 12¼ in. x 4 in.
Photo by Steve Bracken

PAUL LEE
Townsend, Mass.

Tool chest
Mahogany, poplar, holly
32 in. x 17¼ in. 17 in.
Photo by Lance Patterson

101

JOHN P. SCHMIDT
Asheville, N. C.

Pyramid chests
Cherry, purpleheart
10 in. x 10 in. x 9 in.
Photo by Chuck Robertson

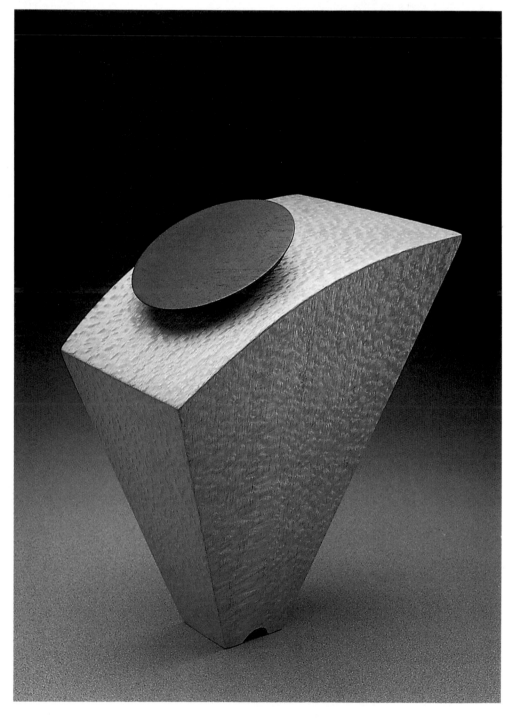

JOHN ERIC BYERS
Philadelphia, Pa.

Lidded vessel
Ebonized mahogany, lacewood
8 in. x 5 in. x 12 in.
Photo by Tom Brummett

TOM STANGELAND
Seattle, Wash.

Jewelry chest
Rosewood, maple, brass, goatskin
20 in. x 9 in. x 16 in.
Photo by Chris Barth

GREGORY W. GUENTHER
Savannah, Ga.

Jewelry box
Bird's-eye maple, Honduras
rosewood, cypress
14 in. x 7 in. x 4¾ in.
Photo by Tim Rhoad & Assoc.

Accessories

RONALD H. REEDER
Seattle, Wash.

Kitchen cabinetry
Alder, walnut, red cedar, fir, holly,
koa, elm, copper
114 in. x 48 in. x 36 in.
Photo by Ronald H. Reeder

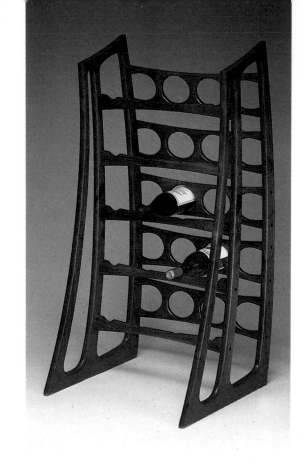

DOUG HURR
Boone, N. C.

Bar
Ebonized mahogany, maple
96 in. x 144-in. dia.
Photo by Doug Hurr

MICHAEL H. deFOREST
Portland, Ore.

Wine rack
Oregon black walnut
21 in. x 21 in. x 43 in.
Photo by Jim Piper

THOMAS R. WOOD
St. Paul, Minn.

Bookends
Mahogany
5 in. x 6¼ in. x 10½ in.

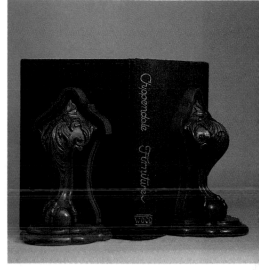

DAVID S. MARK
San Francisco, Calif.

"The Standing Wave Bookcase"
Italian poplar, maple
64 in. x 12 in. x 44 in.
Photo by Moulin Gabriel Studios

MARK BIRMINGHAM
Ft. Collins, Colo.

Folding screen
English brown oak, bubinga
72 in. x 72 in. x 1 in.
Photo by Mac Bauer

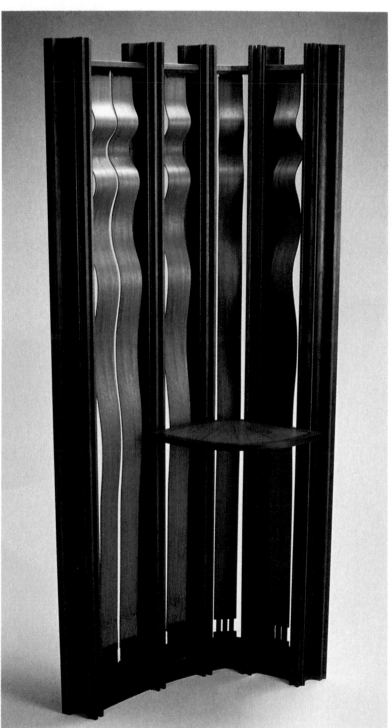

JOHN DODD
Rochester, N. Y.

Room divider
Walnut, bees'-wing narra,
wenge
36 in. x 16 in. x 80 in.
Photo by Woody Packard

PAUL TULLER
Dublin, N. H.

"Hanna No Natsu" entrance screen
Fir, Port Orford cedar, bamboo
11 in. x 35 in. x 59 in.
Photo by Mark Corliss

DOUGLAS A. HASLAM
Calgary, Alberta, Canada

Lamp
Wenge
35 in. x 30 in. x 71 in.
Photo by Chris Thomas

JAMES BACIGALUPI and RICK
NUNES
Campbell, Calif.

Pope's Ambo lectern
California walnut, aluminum,
etched glass
36 in. x 53 in. x 24 in.
Designed by Brother Joseph Aspell
Photo by Dennis Anderson

WILLIAM KEYSER
Honeoye Falls, N. Y.

Baptistry, St. Joseph's Church
Red oak
Photo by David Leveille

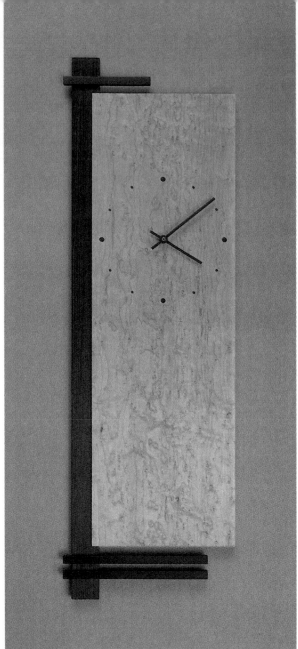

RON CALLARI
Rochester, N. Y.

Wall clock
Bird's-eye maple, Honduras
rosewood, ebony
29 in. x 9 in. x 1 in.
Photo by Micheal Haggart

CHRISTOPHER KUNKLE
Witter, Ark.

Four-fold wall mirror
Honduras mahogany
26 in. x 26 in.
Photo by Robert Billig

CHARLES MARK-WALKER
Cambridge, Mass.

"Wolf Clock"
Pau amarillo
17 in. x 4 in. x 9 in.
Photo by Charles Mark-Walker

TIMOTHY SIMONDS
Chico, Calif.

Hall mirror
Bubinga, macassar ebony,
amaranth, walnut burl, brass
48 in. x 48 in.
Photo by Mike Agliolo

CONNIE and TOM McCOLLEY
Chloe, W. Va.

Basket
White oak, rhododendron
12 in. x 13 in. x 12 in.
Photo by Jerry Anthony

JOHN McGUIRE
Geneva, N. Y.

Casaba sculptural basket
Black ash splint, rosa rugosa,
shagbark hickory
9 in. x 9-in. dia.
Photo by John McGuire

BONNIE KLEIN
Renton, Wash.

Turned earrings
Snakewood, partridgewood,
tulipwood, ebony, olivewood
2 in. x 1 in.
Photo by Mustafa Bilal

WILLIAM L. GOULD
Santa Fe, N. Mex.

Dorpat telescope, ¹/₁₂ scale
Ramon, stained oak, mahogany
11 in. x 11 in. x 14 in.
Photo by William L. Gould

H. TREEN
Haddenham, Cambridgeshire,
England

Beam scales
Boxwood
18 in. x 8 in. x 21 in.
Photo by P. Morley

TOYOJIRO TOMITA
Mikajima, Japan

Bicycle
Zelkova, walnut, Chinese
quince
47 in. x 43 in.
Photo by Giorgio Maggio

STEPHAN TEMPL
Vienna, Austria

Eyeglasses
Rosewood, ebony
Photo by L. Rusch

DANIEL BOTHE
Jamesville, N. Y.

Rocking woolly mammoth
Poplar, black walnut, red oak
66 in. x 26 in. x 40 in.
Photo by Tony Gerardi

ROBERT M. JONES
Dover, N. H.

1912 Model "T" Ford, $\frac{1}{10}$ scale
Poplar, cherry, birch
$14\frac{1}{2}$ in. x $6\frac{7}{8}$ in. x $8\frac{5}{8}$ in.
Photo by David Gill

SUSAN FARRELL
Searsport, Maine

"French Chateau Elaboree"
Baltic birch plywood, poplar
30 in. x 30 in. x 54 in.
Photo by Dan Barba

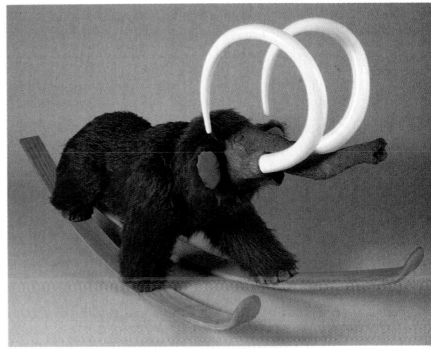

Musical Instruments

JAMES H. BLACKBURN
Minnetonka, Minn.

Lap harp
Cherry, maple, redwood
20 in. x 10 in. x 27 in.
Photo by Wayne Johnstone

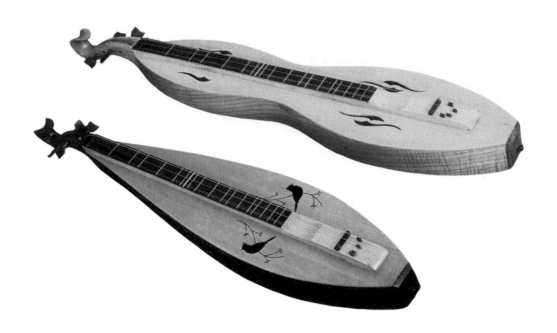

DEE GREEN
Dallas, Ore.

Mountain dulcimers
Oregon walnut, spruce,
cocobolo
40 in. x 7¾ in. x 3½ in.
Photo by Roger Green

KENT EVERETT
Atlanta, Ga.

Mandolin
Sitka spruce, figured maple, ebony,
abalone, mother-of-pearl
27³⁄₁₆ in. x 10¾ in. x 2 in.
Photo by Billy Howard

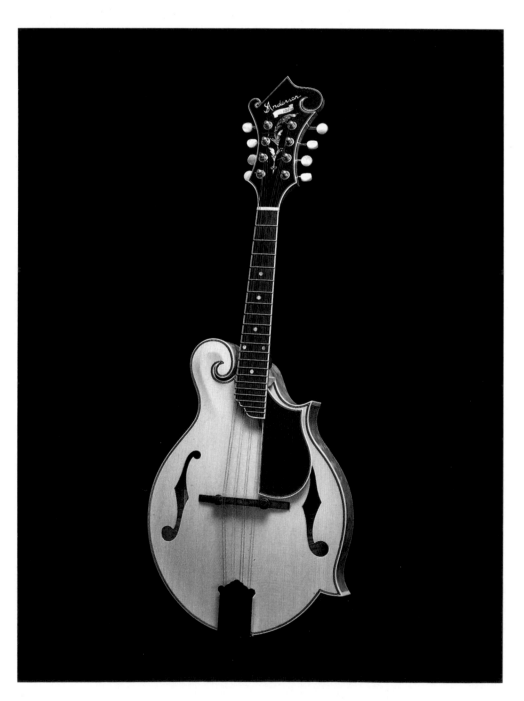

STEVEN ANDERSEN
Seattle, Wash.

Mandolin
Quilted bigleaf maple,
Engelmann spruce
Photo by Chris Eden

ANTHONY KLASSEN
Chicago, Ill.

Guitar #2
Koa, Sitka spruce, mahogany
40½ in. x 16½ in.
Photo by Rick Valicenti

WILLIAM LASKIN
Toronto, Ontario, Canada

Experimental classical guitar
East Indian rosewood, ebony,
German spruce, curly maple
40 in. x 14¾ in.
Photo by Brian Pickell

WALTER STANUL
Malden, Mass.

"Biranium"
Brazilian rosewood, European
spruce, Cuban cedar, ebony
45½ in. x 12½ in. x 3⅝ in.
Photo by Ken Buck

RICHARD SCHNEIDER
Sequim, Wash.

"Jini" recording guitar
Sitka spruce, redwood, Brazilian
rosewood, Honduras mahogany,
ebony
41⅞ in. x 14¼ in. x 4⅜ in.
Photo by Ross Hamilton

RICHARD GOURHAN
Seattle, Wash.

Violin
Spruce, maple, bocote
24 in. x 8 in. x 2 in.
Photo by Rowland's Studio

MAC H. BARNES III
Woodbridge, Va.

Duiffoprugcar violin
European spruce, curly maple,
ebony, various veneers
25 in. x 8¼ in.
Photo by Mac H. Barnes III

DAVID WIEBE
David City, Neb.

Cello
Curly maple, Englemann spruce
Photo by Roger Bruhn

TOM H. ELLIS
Austin, Tex.

Banjo
Curly maple, ebony
38 in. long
Photo by Tom H. Ellis

DICK BOAK
Nazareth, Pa.

Electric bass guitar
45 in. x 12 in. x 1⁵⁄₁₆ in.
Multi-laminate exotic woods
Photo by Mike Krasney

KEN LAWRENCE
Eureka, Calif.

Eight-string bass guitar
Andaman and African padauk,
eastern maple, ebony, brass
48 in. x 15½ in. x 1⅝ in.
Photo by Marc Coates

GREG BRANDT
N. Hollywood, Calif.

Twelve-string acoustic guitar
Brazilian rosewood, curly koa,
western red cedar, ebony,
Honduras mahogany
42½ in. 15 in. x 4⅜ in.
Photo by Emmett Ho

CHARLES M. RUGGLES
Olmsted Falls, Ohio

Pipe organ
Wormy chestnut, butternut,
oak, poplar, sugar pine, cherry
24 in. x 72 in. x 144 in.
Photo by Keith Berr

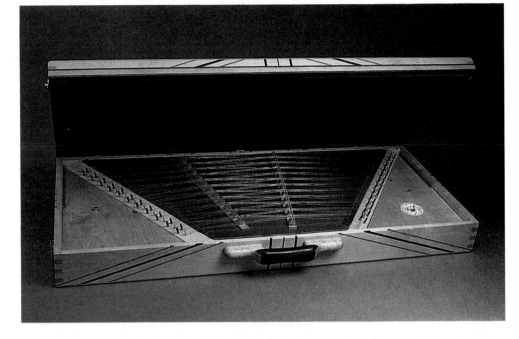

HARLAN OLSON
Bozeman, Mont.

Hammer dulcimer
Maple, teak, purpleheart, walnut,
bocote, rosewood, vermilion
43 in. x 19 in. x 6 in.
Photo by Steven Gray

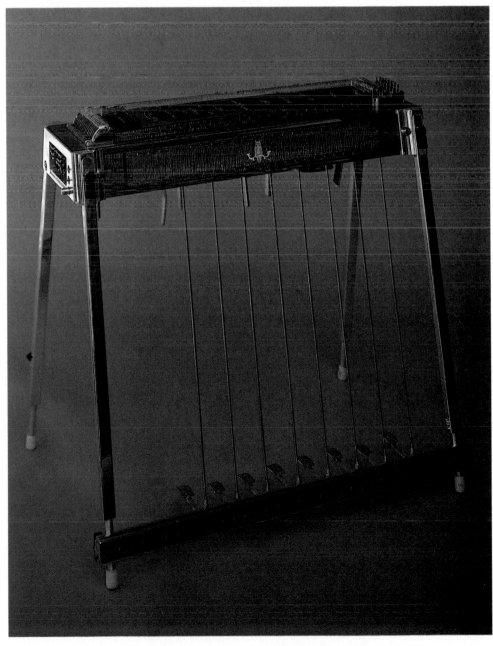

ROBERT GIRDIS
Guemes Island, Wash.

Pedal steel guitar
Koa, ebony, Indian rosewood,
abalone
32 in. x 8 in. x 30 in.
Photo by Ed Littlefield, Jr.

Sculpture

D. G. EIFERT
Algonac, Mich.

Vitrine
Mahogany, birch, walnut, maple
69 in. x 28-in. dia.
Photo by Robert Hensleigh

MADELEINE M. M. McCARTHY
Philadelphia, Pa.

"Vanity"
Ash, wenge, zebra
36 in. x 18 in. x 76-in. dia.
Photo by Tom Brummet

FRANK R. COE
Cambridge, England

Font cover for St. Andrew's
Church
English ash, English brown oak
12 in. x 30-in. dia.
Photo by Roy Smith

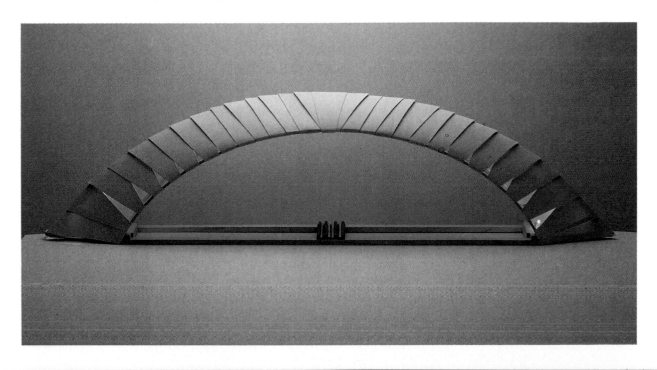

WILLIAM P. MULLER
Crugers, N. Y.

"Siegfried"
Linden
16¼ in. x 4½ in. x 16¼ in.
Photo by William P. Muller

LLOYD MCCAFFERY
Mill Valley, Calif.

"Tecumseh"
Boxwood
3 in. x 2 in. x 4 in.
Photo by Lloyd McCaffery

VICTOR BONDARENKO
Pluckemin, N. J.

"Four-Season Sculpture"
Cherry
54 in. x 10 in. x 32 in.
Photo by Frank Klausz

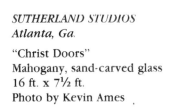

SUTHERLAND STUDIOS
Atlanta, Ga.

"Christ Doors"
Mahogany, sand-carved glass
16 ft. x 7½ ft.
Photo by Kevin Ames

ROBERT I. YOUNG
Big Bear City, Calif.

"Tree Top High"
Ponderosa pine
32 in. x 80 in. x 3½-in. dia.
Photo by Robert I. Young

JOHN C. SHARP
Mineral Point, Wis.

"The Challenge"
Black walnut
23½ in. x 14-in. dia.
Photo by Bill Lemke

DAN LEVIN
East Norwalk, Conn.

Calendar
Honduras mahogany, maple
24 in. x 18¼ in.
Photo by Ron Kupferberg

WILLIAM J. SCHNUTE
Carmel Valley, Calif.

Black squirrel and oak leaves
carved door
White oak, leaded stained glass
48 in. x 4 in. x 80 in.
Photo by Tom G. O'Neal

TREVOR MAYHEW
Thornton Heath, Surrey, England

Beetle box
Laurel, lime, brass, glass
3¾ in. x 2½ in. x 3¾-in. dia.

GEOFF KING
Bruton, Somerset, England

"Teapot Taxi"
English elm, oak, ash, walnut,
bog oak, mulberry
21 in. x 11 in. x 13 in.
Photo by *Woodworker*
magazine

MIKE DARLOW
Chippendale, New South Wales,
Australia

"Oz Durv Tray"
Red cedar
28 in. x 20 in. x 2 in.
Photo by Rowan Fotheringham

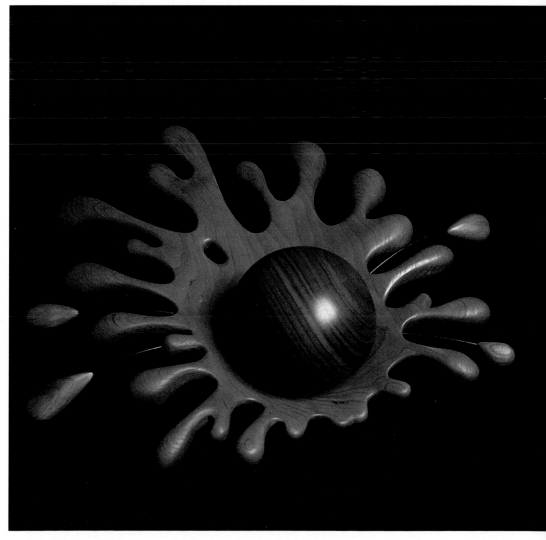

DON MAHIEU
Mineral Point, Wis.

"Splash"
Cherry, pau rosa
10 in. x 10 in. x 2 in.
Photo by Larry La Bonte

139

ABBY MORRISON
West Rockport, Maine

"Diana's Chair"
Yellow birch burl
31 in. x 36 in. x 37 in.
Photo by William Thuss

BOB WOMACK
Cortez, Colo.

Carved bowl and ladle set
Ironwood
16 in. x 10 in.
Photo by Steve Bradley

NORM SARTORIUS
Parkersburg, W. Va.

Spoon
Lilac
10 in. x 2½ in. x ¾ in.
Photo by Jim Osborn

HEATHER HILTON
Atlanta, Ga.

Freestanding bowl
Walnut
15 in. x 28 in. x 14 in.
Photo by Michael McKelvey

ARNOLD R. ALTSHULER
Bethesda, Md.

African crown crane
Birch plywood, walnut, padauk,
mahogany, oak, leather
30 in. x 12 in. x 60 in.
Photo by Schelling Tidmarsh

WILLIAM J. CHILDS
Clovis, Calif.

Carousel lion
Sugar pine
68 in. x 16 in. x 50 in.
Photo by William J. Childs

HAYWOOD NICHOLS
Savannah, Ga.

"Cat on a Table"
Cherry, padauk
24 in. x 12 in. x 44 in.
Photo by Joe Byrd

LEN HOARD
Winnipeg, Manitoba, Canada

"My Son's Little Shoes"
Bird's-eye maple, mahogany,
holly, padauk, walnut
24 in. x 13 in. x 20 in.
Photo by Eric "Fritz" Holland

STAN SCHULZE *and*
TOM SORENSEN
Salt Lake City, Utah

Santa nutcracker
Alder, oak
22 in. x 62 in.
Photo by Dave Newman

ELIZABETH KING
Richmond, Va.

Sculpture with movable joints
Holly
13 in. x 9 in. x 5 in.
Photo by Katherine Wetzel

MARC DAVEY
Seattle, Wash.

Cougar
Jelutong, acrylic paints
38 in. x 16 in. x 20 in.
Photo by Marc Davey

144

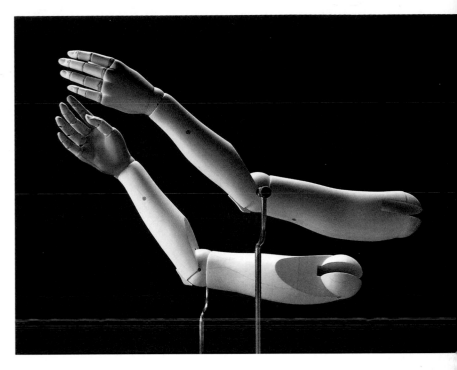

Photos by Scott Landis, except where noted

Design in Context: Woodworkers of the Northwest

by Scott Landis

"Culture," a friend of mine from Oregon likes to say, "never made it over the mountains." According to his theory, when Americans settled the West they left culture behind, dribbled out across the country like gas from a leaky tank. My friend's opinion is shared by many, including the British conductor Sir Thomas Beecham, who is said to have called Seattle an "aesthetic dustbin."

Having lived for a while at the outposts of society, I can understand this point of view. What culture exists on the fringe sometimes seems either hopelessly superficial or derivative. Local

Photo by David Brown

Although much of the region's craft furniture is made of solid wood, styles span a remarkable range from Beth Yoe's painted mahogany chair, above, to Michael de Forest's walnut wine rack, below.

museums in the hinterlands are replete with early chainsaws and wedding dresses from the 1930s—the kind of attic clutter that on the East Coast eventually finds its way into the garbage.

In the Pacific Northwest even the mountains are new, as Mount St. Helens reminded the world nearly a decade ago. And the state of Washington was itself carved out of the Oregon Territory barely 100 years ago, when Seattle was still a small town with big pretensions. Despite a metropolitan-area population approaching 2 million, which is growing by almost 50,000 a year, some would argue that the city is still putting on airs.

A cursory look at the contemporary woodworking of the Pacific Northwest, however, tells a different story. From furniture making to boatbuilding, timber framing, lutherie and carving, there is a richness and vitality of work that equals, or exceeds, anything on the rest of the continent. Almost every type and style of woodwork are represented in this part of the country—usually in some abundance and executed with a high degree of imagination and attention to detail. In short, the craft of woodworking has come of age. If an

area's arts are any measure of its cultural life, then the Northwest is very healthy indeed.

I spent three weeks in early 1989 rooting around in the woodwork of the Pacific Northwest. I visited workshops, museums and galleries from Eugene, Ore., to Vancouver, B. C., trying to understand what made the region so productive. In the process, I hoped to discover what Northwest craftspeople share with the rest of the country and in what ways they are unique.

While I expected to find some homegrown traditions—mainly among boatbuilders and carvers—I wondered whether other aspects of the craft, such as furniture, drew upon references in the environment. Was there a Northwest style? And if so, could it maintain its integrity against a continental drift toward international design? Or might I find the same stuff in New York or Chicago?

Northwest woodworkers, I discovered, have experienced many of the growing pains that are familiar to craftspeople elsewhere in the country. But the relative density and isolation of woodworkers in that corner of the

148

continent make for a kind of crucible of craft. Wherever I turned, I found collaboration to be the rule rather than the exception. Most of the people I met were sustained by a web of informal contacts and trade associations that recalls the region's historic labor movement.

In my peregrinations about the region, I found that the fabled Northwest environment is much more than a colorful backdrop. Over the years, the lush forests and bountiful waters beckoned caravans of 19th-century pioneers along the Oregon Trail as surely as they drew the first settlers across the stepping-stones of the Aleutian Islands. According to Washington novelist Ivan Doig, whose book *Winter Brothers* was to be my companion for the trip, "the west of America draws some of us not because it is the newest region of the country but because it is the oldest, in the sense that the landscape here…more resembles the original continent than does the…Eastern Seaboard…."

Relatively unsullied by industrialization, the Northwest continues to lure the restless and the romantic. Like their predecessors, these latter-day pilgrims typically move to the area first and then look for ways to survive. In the shadow of the awesome

Klamath forest, which once blanketed the coast from California to Alaska with old-growth timber, it's no surprise that a lot of them turn to woodworking.

In Oregon: Strategies for Survival

Trying to sell custom furniture is tough work at the best of times. In a conservative lumber town like Portland, you might have better luck peddling decaf at a truckstop. This situation was exacerbated by the recession of the early 1980s, which brought the Oregon lumber industry to a near standstill. When people stopped buying houses, mills stopped sawing studs, paychecks ceased and elegant handcrafted furniture fell to the bottom of most shopping lists, if it was on the lists at all.

The housing recovery has breathed new life into the Portland economy, and several major public construction projects are underway. The trickle-down has been more like run-off. With few exceptions, the woodworkers I visited had all the work they could handle. It's been a wild ride for those who could hang on.

The craftspeople who managed to survive had adopted several strategies, which I found repeated all over the

Portland's lumber-based economy has rebounded from an early 1980s recession, creating a vigorous market for the crafts-people who survived the lean years.

Northwest. Some charged less for their work in order to get it out the door. Others got by on part-time teaching or the income of a spouse. And almost everyone did at least a little carpentry or cabinetwork—the furniture maker's version of taking in laundry. The extent to which woodworkers no longer have to resort to these practices is generally considered a measure of their success.

A few, like John Economaki, set out to develop a production item that might deliver a steady income without the constant hustle. Ten years ago, Economaki was considered one of the hottest furniture makers on the scene. The fact that he sold over half his work out of state helped to insulate him from the worst of the recession.

That was until 1983, when Economaki launched Bridge City Tool Works. Turning his passion for fine tools to profit, he began selling voluptuous try squares made of rosewood and brass. Applying the same compulsive attention to detail that Economaki formerly lavished on his furniture, Bridge City now makes about a dozen different measuring and marking tools. "Of course the accuracy has to be there," Economaki says, "but I like to think it's the design of the tool that serves as an inspiration to do good work."

Whether you consider it "tool porn" or old-fashioned craftsmanship, it's hard to argue with the results. The company grosses in six figures and employs 20 people. Like Economaki's furniture, most of the tools are also sold out of state, either through high-end tool stores or Bridge City's own catalog.

When we first met four years ago, Economaki assured me that he still wanted to make furniture. "I'm just not so interested in selling it. I don't want to have to work as hard in another twenty years." Predictably, I suppose, he told me last winter that he hadn't built a piece of furniture in three years. In one of our earlier conversations, he put it more succinctly: "I'm in it to make money and we make money. That's the whole idea."

Economaki's success notwithstanding, I couldn't help feeling that most of the woodworkers I met would have considered such a development a bargain with the devil. After all, they had come to the craft to express themselves and to work with their hands, not to fiddle with spreadsheets and oversee employees. If faced with a

John Economaki tired of the craftsman's hand-to-mouth existence. In 1983, he turned his energies to manufacturing fine wood and brass measuring tools.

choice between struggling artistry and a fine widget company, many of them, I felt certain, would have opted for another path.

That's essentially why the Guild of Oregon Woodworkers was formed in 1982. Although the Guild represents only a fraction of woodworkers in the state, almost everyone I met between Portland and Eugene considered the Guild an important factor in the growth and survival of the trade. Sheer distance and two mountain ranges make it impractical to attract members from southern, eastern and coastal Oregon.

About 90% of the state's population lives within 100 miles of Portland, which is roughly the range of the Guild's membership. There are several other similar woodworking associations throughout the Northwest—The Pacific Woodworkers Guild in Vancouver, the Northwest Guild of Fine Woodworking in Seattle and the Northwest Corner Woodworkers Association in Bellingham, Wash.—but it seemed to me, as I toured the region and spoke with several of its members, that the Guild of Oregon Woodworkers was one of the most active.

Bridge City Tool Works supports 20 people on the sales of about a dozen different marking tools and a selection of unusual workshop accessories.

Sam Bush is one of the Guild's greatest spark plugs. He has been an active member from the start and was the organization's second president. Like Economaki and several former presidents, Bush is no longer a woodworker—he's entered the fast-growth field of high-resolution television—but he remains the Guild's self-appointed conscience. He warned the members when he was elected: "I'm going to kick your butts mercilessly." And he's been doing it ever since.

Bush looked around and saw that a lot of his comrades were in trouble. "I realized the problem was *not* with the public, but with the woodworker," Bush recalls. For more than a year Bush kept track of everything he did. He discovered that only half of his time was spent working wood; the rest was spent on business. If members wanted to continue their love affair with the craft, he concluded, they'd have to pay

more attention to phone calls, customers and promotion—the grunt work of the relationship. They would have to calculate all the time that went into their work and charge for it. The Guild invited a lawyer to tell them about business law and an ad man to critique their portfolios.

Bush figured that the public would get the message through increased media attention and an annual show, which the Guild began sponsoring in 1982 at the Western Forestry Center (now the World Forestry Center). The payoff did not come overnight. But last year's Guild show drew more than 4,000 visitors in two and one-half days, almost three times the largest previous attendance. Woodworking shows tend to be a bit like museum exhibitions—the public thinks the stuff is either too precious or too pricey to buy, and woodworkers consider it demeaning to sell. Yet all of the 28 exhibitors at last year's Guild show sold something, and many of them wrote enough orders to keep busy for months.

The show was called Having it Made, and members of the Guild figured they'd come pretty close. Several show ideas seemed particularly inspired. A lucid brochure, handed out at the door, explained how to order work from a Guild member. Folded inside was a ballot with which visitors were asked to select their favorite piece. The ballot was a deceptively simple device. It encouraged visitors to look closely at the work, and it served as a registration form for a handmade door prize. Winning the vote count was almost beside the point. The real value was the names and addresses that everyone added to their mailing list.

Perhaps the most exciting Guild innovation is the 2x4M (Two By Form) Design Challenge. Developed by Jeff Hilber in 1985, it has become an institution at the annual show. The 2x4M challenges members to create a masterpiece from a 2-in. by 4-in. by 8-ft. hunk of plain wood. The photo at right illustrates the creative potential that the contest unleashed. Guild president Ed Mattson told me it was the most enjoyable woodworking he's done, and everyone I spoke with agreed.

In the guise of a no-risk, playful design problem, the 2x4M may turn out to be the Guild's best "hook." The public can relate to a 2x4—especially in Oregon, where lumber is as potent a symbol as potatoes in Idaho. And by creating art from a stud, Guild members are able to communicate the value of their work more effectively than with any amount of slick verbiage. In the bargain, Mattson explained, they promote a conservation ethic by producing something substantial from a common, disposable resource. Mattson hopes that the Guild will direct some of its future energy toward the "ecology" of woodworking—raising consciousness about dwindling sources of supply.

I had only one reservation about the show. How could an open guild, with no membership requirement beyond the annual fee, maintain quality in an unjuried event? No problem, I was assured. Guild membership is self-selecting, and peer pressure sets its own standard. Failing that, an ad-hoc committee will form to address the offender, who, as Sam Bush explained, "generally gets out of the way." A policy of inclusion is admirable, I thought, but ad-hoc committees can turn into lynch mobs. When business

concerns rival social and educational goals, ideals can get caught in the crossfire.

That's exactly what happened to one of the oldest Northwest woodworking guilds, and the result was a nasty family feud. The Washington-based Guild of American Luthiers (G.A.L.), which represents about 2,000 stringed-instrument makers around the country, recently found itself unable to satisfy some of its professional members, who decided to bolt. The G.A.L. appears to have weathered the strife, bolstered, in part, by its strong support in the Pacific Northwest. There are roughly 50 members in Portland alone, and about as many in Seattle. And the organization attracts a diverse blend of amateur and professional instrument makers—from traditional organ builders to electric-guitar makers.

A recent article in the G.A.L. quarterly, *American Lutherie,* hailed Portland as a "lutherie town," and while its stringed-instrument trade may not rival that of Stradivari's Cremona, the city has attracted a critical mass of superb craftspeople. According to luthiers Chris Brandt and Terry

One of the Oregon Guild's most successful promotions has been its annual show at the World Forestry Center in Portland. The show includes the 2x4M Design Challenge, which awards a prize to the craftsman who makes the best piece from one 8-ft. 2x4.

Luthiers Jeff Elliott and Cyndy Burton drove across much of the United States before settling in Portland.

Demezas at The Twelfth Fret, a longtime Portland center for guitar sales and repair, the area's unique energy has a lot to do with the presence of three exceptional talents: Paul Schuback, Robert Lundberg and Jeff Elliott. Schuback's violin apprentice programs, Lundberg's reputation as a scholar and lutemaker and Elliott's superb classical guitars have been a magnet to young luthiers. Much of the new work is obscured by the shadow of the masters, but Demezas assured me that it "is comparable to anything in New York or London."

When I visited Jeff Elliott in the shop and house that he shares with Cyndy Burton, they were finishing two guitars. Elliott was fitting a bridge for one, while Burton was upstairs putting French polish on the other. Their whole house is a workshop. The dining area has been converted to a bench room (and it's kept at a temperature of 65°F for gluing). One of the three bedrooms is an office, and another doubles for guests and finishing. Wood storage and machinery are in the basement. The carpeted living room is used for testing instruments, and guitars are everywhere.

When Elliott finished his apprenticeship in Detroit about 16 years ago and looked around for a corner of sanity in which to work and raise a kid, he drove 10,000 miles in eight weeks until he reached the Northwest. "As soon as we hit the Shasta range [in Northern California]," he recalls, "I started to feel at home." He settled on Portland for its unique cultural and natural environment. The ambient humidity hovers around 50%, which is ideal for his instruments. And a lot of fine native tone woods and ornamental woods, such as cedar, Sitka spruce, yew and holly, grow "right in the backyard."

154

Elliott's rarefied clientele does not exactly grow on trees, but he's managed to build a five-year waiting list that includes some of the world's finest performers—with no advertising. Almost all of his business is out of state and in at least ten different countries. Although Elliott does little else but build concert and recording guitars these days, he survived on a varied diet of repairs, lectures and consultations in his early Portland career. Many of his former apprentices have themselves joined the Northwest guitar community. (Even Richard Schneider, the master to whom Elliott first apprenticed in Michigan, eventually moved to Washington State.)

Perhaps because the local market for handmade instruments is so limited, Elliott and Burton feel that the concentration of luthiers in the Portland area fosters camaraderie, not competition. Events such as the annual Handmade Musical Instrument Show (also held at the World Forestry Center) and the city's open-air market help educate the public to the value of craftsmanship and contribute to the stimulating professional environment. "There are probably 60 instrument makers in the upper Willamette Valley," Burton said, "and somehow we all exist!"

Until recently, Northwest furniture makers have had a rather provincial approach to marketing. But about two years ago, a handful of members of the Guild of Oregon Woodworkers decided to cast their net in a bigger pond. When Mark Hanson proposed that the Guild apply for an opening in Oregon's trade mission to Japan, some Guild members thought he was nuts. Why should they extend themselves abroad when they hadn't figured out how to sell their work at home?

Only 12 members were intrigued enough to pitch in $150 toward plane tickets and expenses, but this was quickly matched by corporate donations. In early October 1987, two months after Hanson's initial proposal, he and Gary Pagenstecher boarded a plane for Tokyo with 27 pieces of furniture and a stack of portfolios.

For six days, Hanson and Pagenstecher hawked Guild furniture, while their fellow exhibitors promoted everything from fish and timber to Oregon wine. At times they felt like decoration or comic relief, but their handmade hardwood products attracted a lot of attention and

Photo by Jeff Elliott

One of Elliott's classical guitars. It's made of African blackwood with an Englemann spruce top.

155

Photo by David Brown

Gary Pagenstecher, Tom Freedman, Michael de Forest, Beth Yoe and Mark Hanson, five Oregon guild members who ventured to Japan to market their work.

appeared to satisfy the Japanese concept of America's pioneer spirit.

The Pacific Northwest has had a long and complex relationship with Asia, dating back to the land bridge between the continents. From the building of the railroads to the strip mining of the Northwest forest, vast human and natural resources have been pumped through the Pacific pipeline. More than 50% of Oregon's exports go to Japan, and the state promotes its wood products throughout the Pacific Rim. On the Tokyo side, a popular Japanese television program, "From Oregon with Love," helps promulgate the mystique of the Northwest.

Banking on what somebody called this "freedomcowboybusiness" and on the Japanese/American trade imbalance, Hanson and Pagenstecher came home and waited. The night I arrived in Portland, Pagenstecher told me, "It's moved incredibly fast and yet, in some ways, excruciatingly slow." After nearly a year of desultory correspondence and two trips to Portland by the president of Epson International, the Guild group finally began to sell furniture. The multinational computer company, which runs a large factory just west of

Portland, was looking for "art furniture" to stock a new gallery and decorate the lobby of its posh Tokyo condos.

By August 1988, when Epson placed its first order, much of the original furniture was no longer available. The Guild group, which was calling itself the Oregon Furniture Designers Guild, had dwindled to three members besides Hanson and Pagenstecher: Michael de Forest, Tom Freedman and Beth Yoe. One soggy Sunday morning, the group got together to discuss the problems and potential in the Japanese project.

"We live in horror," Yoe began, "that they're going to place an order." Part of her fear had to do with the fact that Yoe and Freedman, who live and work together, were in the midst of moving their shop. But the comment had larger implications. "They keep saying they want 'artists,' " she explained, "but then they ask for production."

The numbers were intoxicating. When Epson expressed an interest in several hundred of Hanson's willowy Cheval mirror (top photo, facing page), he figured he could slash the cost of the handle castings from $50.00 to $4.75 a piece. Calculating his construction time for 400 legs and factoring in the production hardware, he arrived at a price. Hanson had built only three by then and, so far, that's all he's sold. Epson got the prototypes for a multi-unit price. It's a situation, Pagenstecher allowed, "we can accommodate only in the very short term." Hanson was more sanguine. By buying their work outright instead of on commission, as most galleries do, "they're bankrolling our future," he said. If nothing else, Yoe concluded, "It's a great boost to our egos."

None of the group was prepared to guess what the future might hold, but I had the sense each dreamed of a different outcome. In six months, Hanson was hoping to make 20 mirrors, while Yoe would be satisfied with six chairs. Michael de Forest wanted to build one desk or table. And all but de Forest were happy to farm out the construction, retaining control over the design. Pagenstecher had already

arranged for a local architectural millwork house, the Charles Grant Company, to build his first Epson chair. (According to the company president, Mike Grant, Pagenstecher got a great deal on the prototype, which took four times as long to build as they estimated for each chair in a production run.) Having no idea what the demand would be, they were grappling with the craftsperson's congenital alter-ego— production. If it grew too large or too quickly, they feared they would lose control of both their business and their work.

The group's work covers a remarkable range, from de Forest's organic furniture made of native Oregon walnut to Pagenstecher's sculptural furniture. With the exception of de Forest, who struck me as the only traditional woodworker in the crowd, the group might be considered the art faction of the Guild. Talent abounds, but they all rely on the

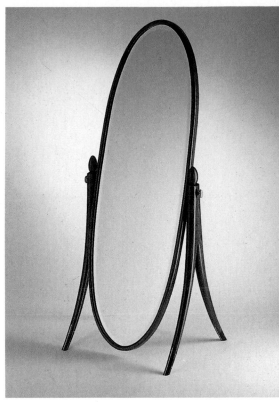

Photo by Joe Felzman studio

Photo by Gary Pagenstecher

Japanese interest in Mark Hanson's walnut and ebony Cheval mirror, above, sent him scrambling for a way to mass-produce what is essentially a one-of-a-kind design. The prototype of Gary Pagenstecher's Egypt chair, left, was among the furniture the Oregon Guild displayed in Japan.

Photo by Eric Griswold

In business since 1971, The Real Mother Goose in Portland is the oldest furniture gallery in the Northwest. Gallery owners Stan and Judy Gillis seek mainstream wooden furniture, shying away from glizty painted work.

income from commissioned furniture or cabinets to finance their more speculative designs.

Pagenstecher, who began making furniture in 1982, has seen his work evolve from an expression of form and line towards what he calls the "sculptural concept." A few years ago, he decided making wooden furniture "was like making matchsticks…it didn't have any reason." So he began to engage themes and issues in increasingly narrative terms. His work is now somewhere between art and furniture and is as likely to be made of metal or granite as wood.

Of the group, Yoe's and Freedman's work struck me as the most international, and perhaps the least likely to sell in Portland. It incorporates a wide variety of materials—Savoy glass, dyed wood and metal—and faux finishes, with Post-Modern and Italian influences. One of a number of husband-and-wife businesses in the Guild, Freedman and Yoe collaborate on most of their furniture. She does the design and he makes sure the joints fit; she does the veneering and he does the finishing; he deals with clients and she handles the books and galleries. "We fight a lot, too," Yoe says.

They've also sunk a lot of energy into promotion and have gotten considerable mileage out of a few pieces. But so far, they've had much better luck placing their work on the East Coast than in Portland, where only one new gallery, Vox, currently shows their furniture.

To find out more about what sells in Portland, I visited The Real Mother Goose, by all accounts the busiest furniture gallery in town. In business since 1971, it is also the oldest in the Northwest. The gallery's main outlet is located one block from Nordstrom's department store, below the city parking garage in the heart of the downtown. (It has another store in a mall on the west side of town and a new, 600-ft. shop at the Portland airport.)

I found the gallery jammed with woodwork. There were at least 50 major pieces of furniture and accessories (plus hundreds of small boxes and gewgaws) and a lot of familiar names among the makers— people I had already seen or planned to see in Oregon and Washington. Influences of James Krenov, Sam Maloof and Arts and Crafts architects Charles and Henry Greene were evident, along with an ample representation of what's popularly known as California roundover work. Only a modified Queen Anne highboy and Evert Sodergren's Tonsu chest (shown on p. 169) made direct reference to older traditions.

By and large, the work was remarkably well built and carefully finished. It was, according to gallery owners Stan and Judy Gillis, "heirloom" furniture. The predominant color was brown. While one or two pieces introduced a sculptural motif, they had a distinctly Northwest flavor and were thoroughly functional. Conspicuously absent was anything that smacked of "art." No paint, no visible metal or plastic and very little inlay. The reason is simple. "It's got to be around long enough for people to accept," Stan Gillis said, and Portland is a conservative market. What's more, only half of the gallery's furniture is sold locally. "The out-of-state people," he added, "want a piece that says 'Oregon'.... We'd like to start showing the art stuff, but it's a tough egg to crack." Gillis also pointed out that one other Portland gallery, Beyond Reason, had already tried and failed.

For a multi-media crafts gallery, The Real Mother Goose devotes an impressive 2,000 sq. ft. to furniture, almost one-third of its total floor space. But when Gillis told me that furniture accounted for only 5% of their gross, I wondered how he justified the commitment. "It's the kind of thing that brings people into the gallery," he said. "But if all I looked at was dollars and cents, I probably wouldn't do it. The main reason is that we love it...and some of our best friends are woodworkers. We've seen them go through the design process and seen their businesses grow. We've been involved from the ground up."

While most of the woodworkers I met considered The Real Mother Goose the best craft gallery in the Northwest, if not the country, very few put much stock in gallery sales. Gary Rogowski, a Portland woodworker who had a handsome linen cabinet and a coffee table on display, told me that "galleries have a way of using up artists." Some of his pieces sell in minutes, while others sit for months. Rogowski figures that he gets five nibbles for every bite. Still, galleries keep the furniture in the public eye, which is better than in your living room. Or, as Ed Mattson concluded, "They're a good place to store your work."

For Portland's Gary Rogowski, below, gallery sales have come slowly. At bottom is one of Rogowski's latest pieces, a vanity made from bloodwood, aluminum and ebonized mahogany.

Photo by Jim Piper

Selling a mix of furniture and carved boxes, Michael and Sharon Elkan are, by most accounts, among the most successful craftspeople in the Northwest.

Michael Elkan is a notable exception. In 1988 he sold more than $25,000 worth of retail furniture at The Real Mother Goose and about half that much in wholesale boxes and mirrors. But then, Elkan's business is exceptional in many respects. He began not as a meticulous craftsman but as a clothing designer and has not only made his peace with production, but embraced it.

In only nine years, Elkan built his business from a mom-and-pop boxmaking trade to a substantial enterprise. He now has five full-time employees (in addition to his wife and brother) and processes two semi-trailer loads of burl a year—roughly 50,000 lb. His boxes, mirrors and a line of furniture sell all over the country in more galleries than Elkan cares to count.

Everywhere I went in Oregon, people pointed to Elkan as the child prodigy, pushed out to perform in front of guests. By any conventional standard of success, he had it made. He makes a unique product, drives an expensive car and has health insurance. When I visited Elkan and his wife, Sharon, last winter, their Florida tans were just beginning to fade.

"I didn't start out to make this a big business," Elkan told me. He and Sharon moved from Philadelphia to escape the frenzy of the rag trade and fetched up on an idyllic 15-acre homestead alongside Silver Creek, about 40 minutes south of Portland. Casting about for something to occupy his time between fashion-consulting jobs, Elkan saw some nifty bandsawn boxes in California. "We could do these," he thought, and began collecting maple root burls. The business grew to include hand mirrors, mirror boxes and furniture, partly as a way to make use of the leftover burl.

The boxes and furniture are more organic than refined—live-edged slabs of outrageous material, presented simply. On a scale from Nakashima to Krenov, Elkan's work is a solid Nakashima—or a little beyond. He makes no pretensions about his skill as a woodworker. When he started he hand-sanded everything. ("I didn't know they had a machine.") He worked with a lot of people and learned as he went. He's more adept chainsawing seat stock from a 4-ft. dia. burl than making casework, so he farms it out. If he needs a drawing, he hires someone to

Gnarly burl edges juxtaposed with smoothly carved surfaces are signature features of Michael Elkan's boxes, left, and furniture, below.

do it. Sharon designs most of the boxes, and he's made at least one of every piece in the shop. But after making 10 or 20 chairs, he said, "Okay, what else can I do?" The 100-ft. long workshop grew like the boxes and the business—without plans.

"They talk about my good business sense, but I've had some great teachers," he said, referring to the street smarts he picked up in North Philly. "A lot of younger guys think they're artists. They do two or three pieces, but they haven't done enough, they don't have any cuts." Boiling his experience to one nugget of advice, he said: "You've got to turn out a product and get it selling—even if you're not making a profit. The concept of selling something is what gets things rolling."

Nobody understood that message more clearly than some of Elkan's fellow woodworkers and Guild members in neighboring Silverton, Salem and Jefferson. One evening last January, I got together in the Elkan kitchen with Michael and Sharon Elkan, Ken Altman, Tom Allen, Michael Jesse and Lewis and Toni Judy. Together, this group forms the core of what I came to

161

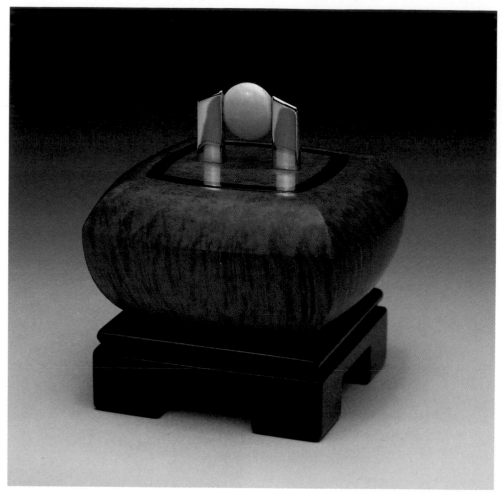

Photo by Ken Altman

Ken Altman, above, is best known for boxes with finely machined sliding dovetails. Lately he's been experimenting with limited-edition work, such as the Greek brier burl and ebony box (top photo). The handle is made of 14-karat gold.

Tom Allen, a graphic artist by training, has had similar success. His company, Joy of Doing, sells more than 1,000 boxes a year—two-thirds of them on the East Coast. He and his wife considered moving closer to their market, but changed their minds when they realized that the cachet of their Oregon address helps sell the work back East. For Allen, the price of success is boredom. "I'm getting tired of doing jewelry boxes," he said. So he's expanded his palette of woods to include a host of local species, eastern hardwoods and exotics. And he's seeking larger, more varied projects such as wall panels, furniture and staircase railings, often done in collaboration with other woodworkers.

People are the Guild's greatest resource, and members share a variety of skills—from marketing savvy to joinery. Allen inlays the tops of Ken Altman's mid-size boxes, which Altman previously had been unable to sell. Altman is one of several Guild members who has built furniture for Elkan, and Altman's wife used to work for Michael Jesse. Jesse, who concentrates mainly on casework, has built blanket chests and headboards for Allen's colorful inlays, and he collaborates with a number of other Guild members. Everyone, it seems, buys walnut from Lewis Judy.

Walnut is not native to the Northwest, but it thrives in the damp climate and long growing season. It reaches enormous size and develops striking grain patterns. I'd heard that Judy had gotten into local walnut, but I didn't realize how far. When I saw him in Silverton, he recounted his recent efforts to buy a 8-ft. dia. specimen from in front of a neighbor's house. To get the tree, Judy bought the house. The limbs, he reports, yielded ten cords.

Judy's gumption is legendary. He boasts the largest small shop around, with a separate router for each bit to save time in production. When he decided to dry his own wood he built not one kiln, but two. And when he figured out that he couldn't afford to sell through galleries, he started his own. The retail display area he added to the end of his shop is furnished like a house, and it's bigger than a lot of New York City apartments. Judy's furniture is straightforward and unsophisticated, with no pretensions to art. He uses solid woods—mainly oak and walnut—with heavily bullnosed corners and a clear finish. I suspect that it's the only

think of as the Silverton nexus. If the Japan group is the cutting edge of the Guild, this group is its ballast.

Like Elkan, Altman and Allen built their businesses on boxes, but are striking out in their own directions. Altman started making his unique sliding-dovetail box about seven years ago. After a few American Craft Enterprises shows, he decided to ship sample boxes to more than a hundred shops around the country. He calculated that the $2,000 investment he made equaled the cost of one show—without the headaches. More than one-third of the shops placed an order, and the list is now practically self-sustaining.

"A lot of people in the Guild have this mentality about wholesale," Altman says. Working alone in a converted garage next to his house, he tries to strike "a delicate balance between keeping busy and being overwhelmed." Income from the production boxes, which retail for around $24, has enabled him to develop a collection of limited-edition boxes, which he plans to market through galleries and shows. These exotic objects, like the one in the photo above, are among the most exquisite that I saw on my journey.

Born and raised in the Northwest, Lewis Judy, left, sells most of his furniture in Oregon. John Brombaugh ships organs all over the country from his shop on the Willamette River in Eugene, Ore. Many, like the one below, are made of fumed white oak with lead-alloy pipes cast and turned on the premises.

handmade furniture many of his customers own. He won the vote count in the 1988 Guild show.

Lewis Judy is one of the few furniture makers I met who was born and raised in the Pacific Northwest. He may be the only one who depends on his Oregon sales. With only one employee, Judy makes all the tables for the Portland-based Old Spaghetti Factory—more than 300 of them last year. That might be a full-time job for most small shops, but it amounted to only 20% of Judy's business. "I think there's a better market here than most people believe," Judy says. "I don't have to go far, and I know who I'm dealing with."

Heading south from Silverton, it occurred to me that the character of the woodwork was beginning to change. The farther I got from the epicenter of the Oregon market, the more specific the work became. While Portland might support a custom-furniture trade, small-town craftspeople have a hard time competing with local furniture stores. I suspect that many try, but few have Lewis Judy's perseverance or success. Many more give up in frustration or look for other markets.

John Fisher's experience confirmed my impression. A graduate of James Krenov's College of the Redwoods program in Ft. Bragg, Calif., Fisher found it difficult to support a family in Eugene by building furniture. (Eugene is a college and lumber town about 110 miles from Portland, with a population around 100,000.) So about three years ago, he began building organs for Brombaugh & Associates. The work is closer in scale to timber framing than

Leroy Setziol, above, used four tons of black walnut to carve the entryway and doors for the chapel at the University of Portland. The entry (top photo) was designed by architect Pietro Belluschi.

(The latter were designed by Pietro Belluschi, the Massachusetts Institute of Technology architect who has been identified with the "Northwest building style.") Setziol recently spent a year carving the 140 6-ft. sq. Alaska yellow cedar panels that encircle the Kaiser Permanente Medical Center in Salem, Ore. He told me he donated his wrists to the project, the biggest of his career.

Half of Setziol's sculpture is commissioned for public spaces, taking advantage of Oregon's and Washington's "1% for the Arts" laws. At least 1% of the cost of every public building must be spent on artwork. His work is in demand, but the prices are still low. According to his wife, Ruth, "he believes that art is for everybody, not just the rich." Setziol advises younger artists to proceed with caution: "Instead of investing in the ego trip—putting high prices on your work—you're better off giving it away."

"Oregon's great claim to glory is wood," Setziol said. "I don't copy nature, but I get ideas from it. A lot of people see coastal things in my work, but it's only partly true. My work is never slick. What the tool does is it. The oil restores the wood to its condition when it was growing…"

what Fisher had been trained to do, but Brombaugh is one of the best in the business. And the job keeps Fisher's own work afloat. He made eight pieces in his shop last year—from small furniture to fireplace mantels. "I haven't met anyone who wants me to do their whole house yet," Fisher said.

Until now, most of the woodworkers I'd met were in their thirties or early forties; few of the "old timers" among them had been at it 15 years. So I found it refreshing to meet Leroy Setziol, a 73-year-old sculptor in Sheridan, about 45 miles southwest of Portland. A former minister and a chaplain in World War II, Setziol gave up the cloth and started working wood in 1951— around the time many of the craftspeople I met were born.

If you've spent any time in the Northwest, you've probably seen his work. It's featured prominently in public spaces all over Oregon and Washington, and its scale is hard to miss. Setziol carved an 80-ft. wall of Honduras mahogany at the Tacoma General Hospital and the four-ton chapel doors at the University of Portland, shown in the photo above.

Washington's Sharper Strivers

If the ocean and mountains are what distinguish the Pacific Northwest from the rest of the country, the Columbia River is what tethers it to the continent. Rising in the Rocky Mountains of British Columbia, the Columbia carves a meandering swath across the Washington interior. As if sensing the ocean nearby, the river straightens out when it reaches Oregon and slices through the Cascades to the sea. For those last few hundred miles it forms the border between Washington and Oregon.

To Ivan Doig, the river defines more than the boundary between two states. In *Winter Brothers,* he describes it as a fault line in the Northwestern psyche: "South of [the river], in Oregon, they have been the sounder citizens, we in Washington the sharper strivers. Transport fifty from each state as a colony on Mars and by nightfall the Oregonians will put up a school and a city hall, the Washingtonians will establish a bank and a union."

At the risk of hanging too large a conclusion on Doig's premise, I thought I saw signs of "sharper striving" among Seattle woodworkers, whose most influential association takes the form of a commercial gallery instead of a guild. One of about two dozen galleries in the city's gentrified Pioneer Square district, the Northwest Gallery of Fine Woodworking is the only gallery in town (and one of the few in the country) to dedicate itself to wooden furniture. Its high standards and prominent profile have identified it with the best of contemporary Northwest work.

First settled in 1851 by five Illinois families, Seattle is no longer the cultural backwater or the best-kept secret it was once considered. With the large presence of Boeing, the aerospace leviathan launched on the wooden wings of the Boeing 80A, the "Pullman of the Skies," the Seattle economy never hit the depths of Portland or Eugene. Today, the city is a center of culture and industry and a gateway to the Pacific Rim. Pioneer Square, which was the site of the first sawmill in Puget Sound, seems an appropriate location for a gallery of handmade woodwork. Only one block away, Yesler Way was the original "skid road," down which logs were dragged to the mill.

The Northwest Gallery is a unique alternative to associations such as the Guild of Oregon Woodworkers, which accommodates both amateurs and professionals. To oversimplify the rationale, amateurs want to improve their work and pros want to sell it. Seattle woodworkers divided roughly along these lines when they formed both a gallery and a guild around 1980 and have gone their separate ways ever since. The guild is inclusive and educational, while the gallery is exclusive and essentially commercial.

Selling comes hard for most woodworkers, and the Northwest Gallery got off to a shaky start. Its 20 original members took turns minding the store, which was attached to one member's workshop. (This fueled the popular fiction that all the work in the showroom was built by a band of elves out back.) After a few months, they hired their first manager, Cheryl Peterson, who convinced them that they couldn't sell woodwork from behind a newspaper. The craftsmen got out of the gallery within a year, and Peterson has been there ever since.

In 1985, the members clarified their cooperative structure, which they modeled after that of an Alaskan halibut fishery. The new by-laws provided for

50 shares of stock, but they held the membership to 30 until recently, when they opened it up to make room for new talent. The gallery now includes 35 members from as far away as Spokane in the east and Bellingham in the north.

Membership benefits are substantial. The gallery holds six shows a year, including an annual group show. Members may propose a one-man show every two years. In addition to their monthly dues, members pay a modest commission of 25% on work sold in the gallery and 15% on referrals, compared to the more conventional 45% and 30% charged to non-members.

"It's not camaraderie that makes our place work," Peterson said. "It's business." And business is looking up. Prices and sales have climbed steadily since the gallery opened. Last year, the gallery grossed more than $600,000 and sold more than half of the 42 pieces in its annual show. "Nine years ago the members were teachers and carpenters," Peterson said. "They did whatever they had to do to get by. Now they're employing other people." Or, as Jonathan Cohen told me, "As the group gets older, fewer and fewer spiritual and aesthetic things come up—it's a matter of money."

Cohen has watched the gallery grow alongside the Seattle market and his own career. "When I started I did anything," Cohen told me. Now, he's booked eight years ahead and turns down almost half of the work that comes in. His hall table, at right, was

Seattle's Northwest Gallery of Fine Woodworking, top, is the only gallery in the Northwest to devote its floor space almost entirely to wooden furniture. Jonathan Cohen's hall table, above, was the best-selling piece at the Gallery last year.

165

Curtis Erpelding, below, is an early member of the Northwest Gallery of Fine Woodworking. He's known for his knockdown furniture designs like the Tensegrity table (bottom photo), which he co-designed with John deChadenedes.

Photo by Mike Zens

the Gallery's best seller last year. Cheryl Peterson told me that Cohen's success has helped raise the ceiling for all local woodworkers—every time he shows his work, the price goes up. Clearly, he would take exception to Leroy Setziol's advice about pricing. "I don't want to give my work away," Cohen said, "or have other people give theirs away."

Still, he clings to a kind of "post-Depression mentality," driving a funky pickup truck and taking his vacations on the cheap. That attitude is shared by Curtis Erpelding, another original gallery member, who confessed that he was his own biggest obstacle. "I'm still living back in '82 or '83 when times were tough," Erpelding said. And he's been slow to realize that there's no difference between hand planing and sanding on most commercial work. "You may bid the job at a good price, but end up losing money just because of your own obsessiveness."

One of Erpelding's abiding obsessions is for things that come apart. Since the knock-down stacking chair he designed in 1982, many of his favorite pieces have been engineered around component parts and mechanical fastenings. But watching them gather dust in the gallery, Erpelding began to appreciate the appeal of Jonathan Cohen's hall table, which can serve a wider variety of functions. And he concedes an inherent contradiction in high-end, knockdown furniture. People won't pay top dollar for a table that comes apart.

The gallery has worked hard to convince Seattle that handmade furniture stays together. Sounding a theme I'd heard at The Real Mother Goose, Peterson told me their woodwork was built to survive "multiple lifetimes of enjoyment." When I noted that many of the same craftsmen show their work in both galleries, Peterson explained that she often trades furniture with what she laughingly called her "Portland warehouse." It's a convenient, informal relationship that enables them to increase the exposure of their furniture and avoid stagnant displays. Some items do better in one place or the other, but both galleries have been instrumental in establishing woodwork as a serious art form and in educating the Northwest market.

Compared to the Real Mother Goose, the Northwest Gallery crams more work and, in some respects, more diversity into a smaller space. The gallery also makes room for sculpture, like Michael Davock's female torso and quasi-functional "room jewelry" by Emmett Day (photos at right and below). Glancing around the showroom, I couldn't help noticing that people—men especially—treat the place like a shrine. But I was struck again, as I had been in Portland, by a kind of homogeneity amidst the diversity. In the face of so much elegant work it seems almost churlish to say that I found myself yearning for something else—something a bit less precious, less fussy and less self-conscious. Something I could live with myself.

When I inquired about the dearth of period furniture, Peterson explained that the focus of the gallery is contemporary. "Not that period furniture isn't fine woodworking," she said, but there simply isn't room to show both. She added that the jury that selects work from non-members bases its decisions on quality of construction, pricing and sales potential rather than aesthetics. But more than one gallery member told me about applicants whose work had been rejected for

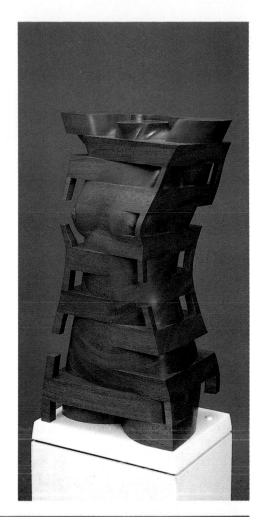

Photos by Greg Krogstad

The Northwest Gallery of Fine Woodworking finds room for sculpture and high-end art furniture. Michael Davock's female torso in mahogany, above left, and Emmett Day's cylinder desk in ebony, rosewood and mother of pearl, left, are two examples.

George Levin's tall-case clocks are departures from the predominantly contemporary design prevalent in the Northwest.

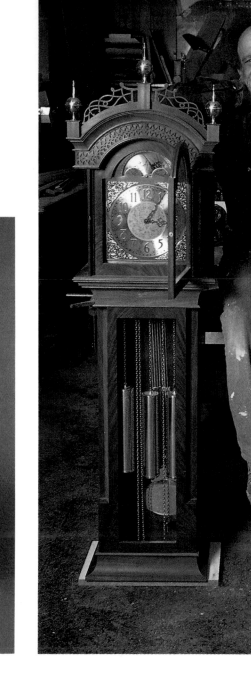

Photo by Greg Krogstad

Judith Ames' solid-wood functional furniture reflects her interest in simple, Shaker-inspired design.

being "derivative." This seemed a curious distinction, considering the pervasive influence of James Krenov in so much gallery work. Even Emmett Day's extravaganzas make obvious reference to the Art Deco style of Jacques-Emile Ruhlmann, and Judith Ames' work emulates Shaker simplicity.

Peterson put me in touch with George Levin, whose tall-case clocks (shown above) were among the few examples of unabashed period furniture I saw in the Northwest. Levin is a retired engineer and not a gallery member, but his high-style Federal and Art Deco pieces are lovingly crafted. I

couldn't help wondering: If it were possible to purge contemporary design of such influences, would anyone care to own the result?

Among the bulk of gallery fare, I found Evert Sodergren's Tonsu chest, shown on the facing page, to be refreshingly direct and unpretentious. Sodergren is an anomaly among members of the gallery. A fourth-generation Seattle cabinetmaker, Sodergren learned from his father, to whom "a contemporary piece of furniture was non-existent." And he admires his grandfather most of all, who was a farmer/woodworker in Sweden: "I like the idea of being able to do anything that comes along."

While Sodergren told me that the gallery was "the best thing to happen to Seattle," he took strong exception to its preoccupation with contemporary work. "People are trying awfully hard to be different," he said. "I'm not into that. I think you can separate the men from the boys in a damned hurry if you start duplicating the masters' work." Not at all troubled by the fact that the Tonsu is a take-off on a traditional Korean design, Sodergren added: "There isn't anybody here who's doing anything fresh. But that's all right, we all have to draw from the past—even if it's only the immediate past."

Sodergren taught furniture design at the University of Washington and was closely allied in the 1950s with a group of Northwest artists and architects. In 50 years of furniture making, Sodergren said, "I've gone through lots of phases." But he describes them in terms of techniques or materials, rather than design.

In the early 1970s, Sodergren discovered that by altering the size of the carcase and the layout of the drawers, he could make a Tonsu to suit any purpose. It works well as a dresser, a sideboard, a night table or a bar. "It's more versatile than anything I've ever made," Sodergren says, and several hundred customers agree. "Every time I do a run," he told me, "I say it's my last." But he enjoys making the puddled bronze castings and finds that the casework is good practice for his apprentices. Sodergren admires the tenacity and perfection of some of his younger colleagues—particularly Emmett Day. But he cautions: "You gotta know when to stop."

Photo by Neil Planert

Evert Sodergren's Tonsu chest is based on a traditional Korean design.

Photo by Chris Eden

As is the case elsewhere, craftspeople in the Northwest pool their resources and share shops. Clockwise from top left: Ross Day, Bill Walker, Michael Davock and Stewart Wurtz share quarters in Seattle.

Knowing when to let go is the craftsman's perpetual burden. I found it most persistent among younger, highly trained furniture makers like Stewart Wurtz, Ross Day and Bill Walker, who share a Seattle workshop with sculptor Michael Davock. Most of the people I met were self-taught or the product of an informal apprenticeship, which may account for their overwhelming fascination with novelty, but Wurtz, Day and Walker are among the best-educated woodworkers in town. Wurtz is a graduate of the Boston University Program in Artisanry, Day spent a year at Gompers, a Seattle community college, and he and Walker attended

the College of the Redwoods. Their furniture is as fine as anything around, but I wondered how all this schooling stood up to the marketplace, especially in Seattle, where excellent work threatens to be the norm.

"Student work is *over*worked," Day said. The standard of perfection that's encouraged in most craft programs offers a noble path to starvation unless it's tempered by reality. For Wurtz, Day and Walker, that means working more quickly, knowing when to put aside the scraper and rent a time-saver and finding ways to subsidize their obsession. "It takes time to develop a coherent sense of design," Walker said. "It's important to give yourself as much of a break as you can afford. I ended up building a lot of kitchens, and a couple of pieces that were as good as I could make them." He has allowed himself five years to "balance the equation," and every year it shifts in his favor.

The group is also aiming for the right mix of commissions (secure but restrictive) and speculative work (risky but stimulating). Wurtz thrives on the latter, while Walker told me: "I enjoy designing with one person in mind, rather than working long distance." After making several pieces for the same client, the job gets easier. Not coincidentally, Walker was the only member of the shop who did not belong to the Northwest Gallery.

"Seattle is a great town," Walker said. "Not only the clients, but the community. It's nice not to work in a vacuum." And compared with Mendocino, where Walker made guitars after graduating from school, Seattle is a lot less competitive. Still, Day added, "this is such a solitary way to earn a living." In the shop they share much more than equipment. They collaborate on large projects, offer a fresh eye on design problems and provide moral support. "We're all still chasing the dream," Day said.

For at least one gallery member, the Seattle woodworking enclave proved to be a hindrance rather than an advantage. Michael Strong began making furniture at Seattle's University of Washington in 1975, but he quit the city to establish his own identity. After a stint in the small town of La Conner and six months at Karl Malmsten's studio in Sweden, Strong settled in Bellingham, about 90 miles north of Seattle and not far from the Canadian border. With a population of 50,000 and an economy built on wood, fish

and Western Washington University, Bellingham appealed to Strong as a suitable cultural eddy in which to develop his own "vision." (Bellingham may soon undergo a dramatic transformation due to the U.S.-Canadian Free Trade Agreement and the city's designation as the new terminus for the Alaska ferry.)

About a decade later, Strong's identity and reputation are secure. He's done a lot of one-off pieces over the years, but is best known for his portfolio of chair designs. "I'm not going back to Seattle," Strong told me last winter, "but I could go back now."

One of the things that appeals to Strong about Bellingham (and the Northwest in general) is its youth. "There's no tradition to pay homage to," he explained. "You don't have to be respectful of the Shakers because there were no Shakers here." Still, it's not as though Strong designs in a vacuum, he just works with a broader palette. His Calyx chair, at right, makes reference to Scandinavian tradition, his Fan chair relates to Hepplewhite, his Hesta chair is reminiscent of the Greek klismos and his popular fireside stools suggest an oriental expression of curved and straight lines. His latest series, the Northwest easy chair, recalls the Arts and Crafts aesthetic of William Morris and the architects Charles and Henry Greene.

In its design and concept, Strong's adjustable Northwest chair, a detail of which is shown at bottom right, is something of a departure. "I've always made very curvaceous things," Strong said, and this is his first planar chair. It's also the first time that he designed a chair to suit a market. "Woodworkers typically make things first," Strong

Photos by Rod Burton

Strong's Calyx chair, above, reflects the influence of a half-year spent at Karl Malmsten's design studio in Sweden. At left is a detail of his Northwest chair, the first piece he designed to suit a particular market.

Artwood, a Bellingham cooperative gallery, shows the work of professionals and amateurs. The Windsor chair at right was made by Jim Hume, a professional race-car builder.

Photo by David Scherrer

Vernon Liebrant turns outsized bowls, mostly from local wood and salvaged material from his own apple orchards.

noted, "and then try to find someone to buy them." Ironically, the market he identified was in Seattle, where a lot of people live in one-story and two-story Arts and Crafts bungalows.

The Northwest Gallery in Seattle has been "a godsend" for Strong, who laments that Bellingham "doesn't have enough doctors" to support a big-city traffic in custom furniture. But he finds it a better outlet for one-of-a-kind accessories than for whole suites of furniture. To furnish an entire room or a house, he explains, people are more likely to go to a furniture store. Strong hopes that the easy chair will provide entry into furniture stores, about the only major market he has yet to explore. "You tinker with a business like you tinker with a design," Strong says.

In May 1988, Michael Strong and a group of Bellingham-area woodworkers pooled their resources to reach the local market. About 20 members of the Northwest Corner Woodworker's Association gutted an old health-food store in downtown Bellingham (known locally as the "hippy building") and opened Artwood, a cooperative furniture gallery. Artwood is a scaled-down version of the Northwest Gallery, with even more exposed joinery and oiled hardwoods. Its conservative mix of furniture and accessories is an appropriate reflection of the local craft and market.

Most, but not all, of the work in Artwood is produced by full-time, professional woodworkers like Michael Strong. But I found some excellent amateur examples, such as Jim Hume's

square-spindle, Windsor rocker (shown at left) and Vernon Liebrant's oversize bowls (shown below left). (Hume builds custom racing cars for a living, and Liebrant is an apple grower and former sawmill operator.) Liebrant is a "home-grown" turner and a member of the American Association of Woodturners, which is active in Seattle. He turns most of his bowls from local woods, salvaged from his orchards and neighboring yards and woodlots. Even his jumbo lathe is a classic "found" object, a welded patchwork of scrap iron from old sawmills.

Perhaps because of its youth (or Bellingham's small-town atmosphere), Artwood retains many of the vestiges of a guild association that the Northwest Gallery seems to have lost. For several of the people I spoke with who are sprinkled around the hills and farmland outside of town, Artwood is more than just another consignment outlet. It also fulfills an important social and educational function. For Lance and Karen Howell, of Maple Falls (shown in the photo on the facing page), these may be the gallery's greatest assets. "We've learned a lot from the other members," Karen Howell explained. "Before the gallery came along, we would just do things wrong five hundred times."

The Howells make looms and Shaker-style boxes in the shadow of Mount Baker, about 45 minutes northeast of Bellingham. While there are woodworkers in all directions, distance and the demands of country living provide few enough excuses to get together. No strangers to isolation, Lance and Karen and their teenage daughter, MayLinn, moved to Washington from Alaska in the late 1970s, where they spent most of that decade fishing and sawing salvaged driftwood on the ocean beaches. Karen built one of her first looms in Alaska out of beach logs and little bits of hardwood that floated down the Stikine River or washed ashore from old shipwrecks. An order for a $600 loom in 1978 paid for a table saw, a sander and the Maple Falls workshop the Howells have used for ten years. They began making Shaker boxes a few years later to fill in the "months of unstructured time" between fishing forays up the coast.

The boxes are nicely made Northwest variations on the Shaker original, with snazzy bookmatched tops. "The old Shaker boxes were the plastic buckets of their day," Lance says, "so we spruced them up." While they're not as understated, refined or authentic as other reproductions I've seen, Lance says simply: "Woodworkers might like theirs, but the general public buys ours." Many of the other woodworkers I met were trying to promote themselves as artists, but Lance had no such pretensions. "This is a manufacturing business," he said, "not an art. And we don't set our bait for rich people. For me, it's a big achievement for our Shaker box to be in a house that's full of junk."

What's more, the Howells find it hard to justify the use of exotic woods that has become so prevalent in the Northwest, as it has around the country. The use of ivory, they consider abhorrent. "A beautiful table stops looking beautiful," Lance told me, when he reckons the wages earned by the people who cut the wood and the devastation wrought on distant forests.

The Howells enjoy the challenge of creating simple, solid furniture out of local wood—wood they can vouch for. And Lance often takes part in the milling, sometimes trading furniture for lumber. When I visited Lance and Karen last January, they had just taken delivery of two truckloads of walnut from a friend's mill. They use mainly local walnut, bigleaf maple (the detritus of logging operations), alder and eastern cherry, which they're trying to phase out with local substitutes.

Their business plan is measured not so much in terms of outlets or units sold as in acres of new trees, which get mulched with workshop shavings. Lance is doggedly covering their property ("and sometimes I spill over the borders") in black cherry, oak, walnut and American chestnut—all species that local foresters assure him won't grow in the area. Eventually, he hopes to establish ten acres of sustainable woodlands.

Still, their Maple Falls location does not seem to have impeded business. The Howells make about 1,600 boxes a year, which they sell through a couple of dozen gift shops around the country (the Smithsonian buys roughly one-quarter of their production). Many of the shops, Karen says, "have no idea we're just two people," plus MayLinn, who blisses out on loud rock music while she waxes.

Like the boxmakers of Silverton, Ore., the Howells' success may be their greatest challenge. They recently poured the concrete foundation for a

new workshop, more than triple the size of the one that built their business. And the business has brought them another mouth to feed—their first part-time employee. Lance figures they work about 30 hours a week in the summer and 45 hours a week through the fall. "That's why we quit fishing," he says. He plans to keep a growing pace until the new shop is outfitted with a sander and dust collector. "But personally," he adds, "forty hours a week is too much. We want to do more things in the day that aren't related to money."

Photo by Rod del Pozo

Lance and Karen Howell atop a stack of freshly sawn walnut. The Howells use local woods in their looms and in Shaker boxes, which they sell through gift shops around the country.

Seattle's Center for Wooden Boats, directed by Dick Wagner, above, is home port for some 1,500 wooden-boat enthusiasts.

Along the Waterfront

The mountains and forests of the Northwest are an important aspect of the region's character, but water really settled the country. In Oregon, the population gravitated inland to the fertile basins of the Columbia and Willamette rivers and away from the unwrinkled coastline, which provides few safe harbors. Farther north, the islands, estuaries and fjord-like intrusions of Puget Sound have nurtured maritime culture for thousands of years. As the primary means of getting around on the water, boats have a special status among all wooden objects in the Northwest.

Sooner or later, any serious boat enthusiast is bound to run aground at The Center for Wooden Boats in Seattle. In its various incarnations as museum, school, publisher and boat livery, the Center is the focal point for the repair and restoration of the wooden-boat heritage of Puget Sound. It is not the only repository of the tradition, but it is one of the most industrious. More tugboat than schooner, the Center has nudged its membership through 20 years of economic difficulties and shifting political currents. When I visited the Center last winter, I discovered that its influence extends well beyond the "hard-core boat nuts" who brought it to life. I had the feeling it was entering the Seattle mainstream.

The Center is itself afloat—a labyrinth of small pavilions and planked catwalks, anchored at the south end of Lake Union. (Located on the edge of downtown, this freshwater lake is home to a considerable houseboat population and much of Seattle's marine service industry.) I reached the Center, as most landlubbers do, by descending a steep gangplank from shore. Hunkered down modestly between the cavernous Naval Reserve Drill Hall and a nautical Burger King, it is easy to miss. I overheard the Center's director, Dick Wagner, instruct an inquiring caller: "It's like Shangri-La. You'll find it when you've earned the right to find it."

Wagner is the director, chief navigator and guiding spirit of the Center for Wooden Boats. Even its floating structure is a synthesis of his architectural training and passion for boats. While the Center functions, in part, as home to a growing collection of historic watercraft, it is much more than a museum. Its purpose, Wagner explained, is to "get people interested and involved in small-craft heritage through participation. I'd rather have people doing something than just gawking."

The Center's ambitious program is a measure of Wagner's commitment and success. It hosts an annual three-day wooden-boat exposition, regattas in the spring and fall and seminars on diverse nautical subjects—from lofting to bronze casting and marine photography. The Center offers week-long boatbuilding workshops for student-built projects—like Simon Watts' lapstrake Petaluma rowing shell and Jerry Stelmok's Maine guide canoe. The finished boats usually join the Center's thriving rental fleet, which numbers more than 40 craft.

"Eleven years ago," Wagner wrote in 1987, "we began as a group of fanatics who met in a houseboat living room to map a dream." The dream has come a long way from the boat livery service that Dick and his wife, Coleen, operated from their Lake Union houseboat. At the end of the dock is the latest addition—an education center that will house a library, offices and a 100-seat auditorium. The new building is designed to evoke the ambience of Seattle's early lakefront and the livery trade that inspired the Wagners in the first place. Like the Center, which now has about 1,500 members, the dream has expanded to include an ambitious plan to turn the entire south end of the lake into a multi-use maritime park. "It's no fun," says Wagner, "unless it's an adventure."

"Everybody who's building a wooden boat," Wagner says, "is helping to carry on our heritage." He estimates that there are about 50 to 75 professional wooden-boat builders between Olympia and the San Juan Islands. But very few of them, he explains, are building traditional, plank-on-frame wooden boats. Most survive on repairs or trimming out glass hulls. Carl Brownstein, Wagner points out, is one of the exceptions. "In 1978, plus or minus six months, ten thousand people in their early twenties decided 'I want to be a boatbuilder," Wagner says. "Carl stuck to it."

The trip to Carl Brownstein's shop is a little like a visit to rural Maine. To get there, I traced a circuitous path along progressively narrower fir-lined roads that skirt the Totten inlet. This tidal reach is near the bottom of Puget Sound at the throat of the Olympic peninsula—the 85-mile-wide headland that separates the sound from the sea. (George Vancouver's navigator, Lt. Peter Puget, somehow missed Totten inlet when he charted the waters of the sound in 1792.) The muddy ruts end at a clearing in Brownstein's nine-acre woodlot, with an aluminum house trailer and two large, plastic-covered boat sheds—the unlikely headquarters of Rights O' Man Boatworks.

Under plastic roofs that were bellied with rainwater, Brownstein toured me around two hulls in progress. "I don't think there's anybody else building as many wooden boats or as big," he announced in a tone that was more matter-of-fact than boastful. In the first shed was a 36-ft. cat yawl, modified from a Chesapeake Bay design, which suits the shallow water, narrow inlets and sudden squalls of Puget Sound. Next door was an elegant 39-ft. John Seward cutter (shown at bottom right), built from what Brownstein called a virtual "rainforest" of mahogany, teak and oak atop four tons of lead keel. Later on, I visted a third Brownstein boat in a backyard shed about 30 miles away. That one—a handsome 30-ft. Lyle Hess cutter (fir on oak, with a teak deck and mahogany cabin)—had been three years in the making and was still on blocks.

With the help of two assistants, Brownstein has built about 85 boats in ten years—an impressive statistic considering that many of them seem to have crossed the fuzzy meridian that separates boats from ships. He does

build smaller craft—an occasional lapstrake Rangely and some 21-ft. racing gigs—but his current projects are in the one-to-three year range, and still going.

Like a lot of Northwest boatbuilders, Brownstein traces his boat roots to the East Coast, where he learned to build kayaks and "crude things" at a scout camp in rural Maine. He discovered real boats at Evergreen State College in Olympia, where he worked on a 38-ft. cutter at the historic H. A. Long Boat Works. Long's yard and two months of cutter framing went up in smoke when a steambox fire got away. Hank Long retired, but an undaunted Brownstein enrolled in the boatbuilding program at L. H. Bates Vocational Technical Institute in Tacoma. In an interview for *Shavings,* the bimonthly newsletter of The Center for Wooden Boats, Brownstein noted that when Long retired after the fire, "I had some idea that I would take up where Hank left off. Otherwise the world might end up short a boatbuilder."

Since he set up shop in 1977, Brownstein has learned two hard lessons: "People who want wooden boats want to be involved with building them," and "all my customers pick a project that's at the extent of—or generally beyond—their means." These realities have sobering implications for wooden-boat builders everywhere. Brownstein survives by dint of perseverance and flexibility. While he prefers to finish his boats from the

Carl Brownstein (bottom photo) with a 39-ft. Seward cutter. Brownstein has built 85 boats in ten years, an astonishing output for a three-person shop. Below is a 21-ft. sloop-rigged Sharpie that Brownstein built in 1981.

inside out, many of his projects are "owner assisted." He often leaves the fitting out and finishing to his customers or works alongside them, building and teaching as he goes.

The scale of his projects is daunting, but Brownstein dwells on the details—the bronze floor fastenings, the neatly chamfered butt blocks and the trim of the transom. Reciting a familiar theme, Brownstein admitted that he gives his customers more than they expect, or pay for. As for making a living, he snorted and gestured at the trailer and disreputable-looking boatsheds around him, "well, you see what it is…but we're alive."

From Brownstein's shop, I followed the Hood Canal north to Port Townsend, where Puget Sound joins the Strait of Juan de Fuca. Primly

Many of Port Townsend's craftspeople have come up through the marine trades, including carousel carver Bill Dentzel.

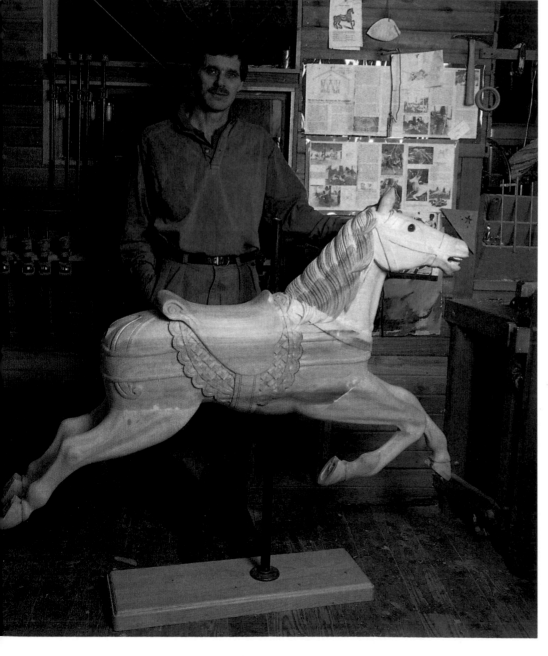

perched on a bluff overlooking Admiralty Inlet, the town that once collected 19th-century sailing ships and settlers as with a landing net now lures wooden-boat enthusiasts. Alas, Port Townsend pinned its hopes on a railway that never came and was flash-frozen in the 1890s.

Redemption comes in odd packages. In Port Townsend, it never took a shape that the original town fathers could have envisioned. But in a curious way, the town's seclusion in time and at the end of its own small peninsula strikes a potent chord in craftspeople of all persuasions. It struck me as a microcosm of the Northwest, a place where people come first to live, and then figure out how to survive—an "unintentional intentional community," as one resident I met put it.

To the owners and builders of wooden boats, who themselves reside in a kind of cul-de-sac, it is particularly attractive. (I'm told that, for many of the live-aboard crowd, it's the only sane landfall this side of Alaska.) There are several boatbuilding companies as well as spar, oar, block and sailmaking shops, a specialty lumberyard and a pattern shop and foundry.

Two of Port Townsend's great attractions are the Wooden Boat Foundation and the Northwest School of Wooden Boatbuilding. Together, they perform many of the same functions as The Center for Wooden Boats in Seattle. The Foundation adopts a more public profile, with its newsletter and annual festival, while the Northwest School is a training ground for builders from around the world. (Carl Brownstein is one of a dozen Puget Sound craftspeople to conduct workshops at the school each year, drawing students from as far away as Tanzania.)

The Northwest School offers a six-month crash course in the "environment of traditional wooden boatbuilding," with an emphasis on the traditional. No cold-molded epoxy work is allowed. "It's not as though we're against it," I was told, "it's just that's not what the school is here for." The school teaches the "scientific" method of traditional boatbuilding championed by Bob Prothero, who founded the school in 1980. Prothero died in 1986, after training more than 200 students. Many who came never left, but I wondered if there were enough wooden boats around to hold them. Jeff Hammond, the school's head instructor (and hand-picked successor to Bob Prothero) responded quickly: "There's a guy in town right now looking for three boatbuilders."

Many of the people I met in Port Townsend have a connection with wooden boats, even if they no longer build them. For some, like carousel carver Bill Dentzel (photo facing page), boatbuilding is something to fall back on when he needs the work. Dentzel, who comes from a long line of carousel carvers, has been carving a menagerie of animals since 1981. Like boats, he explains, carousels require a facility with ironwork, machinery and painting, as well as an understanding of balance and three-dimensional form. Dentzel sells "living-room animals" to make money, "but my true energy," he said, "is toward the carousel as a whole mechanism, with people riding on it. It's a magic thing." But you can't just build a carousel and expect it to thrive. "Carousels are like pet animals," he said. "If you don't have them in the right place they won't live."

For others, like timber-framer Doug Nash, the water and boats are what brought him to town. Nash landed a job and a place to live within two hours of his arrival in 1977. He worked in the marine trade for seven years until taking up with a local timber-framing company—mainly in order to build his own home.

Nash's timber frame, which is shown in the photo at right, blends easily with the Victorian vernacular architecture of Port Townsend. Parts of the building come from all over the country. Its Douglas fir beams are from Oregon, the stress-skin panels come from Vermont, the Rumford fireplace design originated in New England and the custom windows were built on San Juan Island across the strait. But the lofting techniques Nash used to assemble the curved, laminated beams in the gables are right out of the boatshop. In fact, he traded work on a 32-ft. Chris-Craft for the posts, which were turned by Earle Wakefield, Nash's former boss and the venerable founder of Admiral Marine Works, a mainstay of Port Townsend's commercial boatbuilding industry.

The company Nash works for and that built his house is Charles Landau's Timbercraft Homes. Like many craftspeople I met in the Northwest, Charles and Judith Landau fell into their trade. They followed the instructions in a book when they built their first timber-frame house. Now

they have eight full-time employees, they're booked six months ahead and they raise 10 to 12 frames a year from Alaska to New Mexico. Alaska is readily accessible from Port Townsend and, until the oil economy went flat, Landau did a good business there. He found he could ship precut frames by barge and still beat the local competition. In 1987, he went even farther afield and raised a 3,400-sq. ft. timber frame in downtown Tokyo.

Timbercraft's houses reveal a strong New England Cape Cod influence. But Landau told me that he and Judith, who designs many of their frames, were developing their own style, based on Western architectural influences such as climate, geography, oriental design and the work of the architects Charles and Henry Greene.

Landau is also very active in the Timber Framers Guild of North America, and is a founding member of the Western Regional Timber Framers Guild. One of the Western guild's top priorities is to halt the depletion of old-growth timber in the Cascades. As mill after mill is devoted to the export trade, it has become increasingly difficult for the small local builder to find good material. "The Northwest is the only place in the world where Douglas fir and cedar trees like these can grow," Landau said. Wouldn't it be ironic, he asked, if just as the technology of building houses that last 500 years comes of age, the old-growth timber were to disappear?

Doug Nash, at right in the photo above, began his career as a boatbuilder. At left is Charles Landau, the owner of Timbercraft Homes.

Photo by Charles Landau

Nash drew on boatbuilding techniques to lay out and laminate this curved beam for the gable end of his timber-frame house in Port Townsend.

Vancouver Island carver Tim Paul at work on a 26-ft. yellow cedar totem. The pole is for Canada's new National Museum of Man in Ottawa.

The Wooden Culture

Irony is not lost on native Northwesterners. For when people speculate about a lack of culture west of the mountains (as I did at the beginning of this essay), they undoubtedly shortchange the original culture, which preceded the arrival of Captain James Cook by some 10,000 years. Theirs was truly a wooden culture. Wood was the primary material used in native houses, boats, tools and even some clothing (hats were made from spruce roots and garments were woven from shredded cedar bark). Wood permeates their ritual artwork.

Northwest Coast art is in the midst of a renaissance not unlike the craft revival of the 1960s and 1970s, but it, too, is loaded with irony and contradiction. Like a tree replanted by its branches, the art is helping to resuscitate the culture, which was yanked out by the roots a century ago. And although whites precipitated its decline, they've played an important role in its preservation and rebirth.

In a recent newsletter published by The Legacy (a Seattle gallery of Northwest Coast Indian art), John McKillop recalled his first meeting with Henry Hunt, one of the patriarchs of the foremost clan of native carvers. Hunt was working in a carving shed behind the Provincial Museum in Victoria, B. C. Above him on the wall was a *Playboy* centerfold, her airbrushed contours neatly but not entirely overlaid with traditional Northwest Coast designs—the distinctive, convoluted scrollwork of bold line and interlocking form that decorates native artwork in the region. Distracted by the multi-cultural collaboration, McKillop found it hard to concentrate on the bemused Hunt, who eventually asked: "What's the matter, never seen flat design before?"

To many Northwest Coast carvers, the Provincial Museum has been the keeper of the flame. It houses an extraordinary collection of masks, totem poles, kerf-bent boxes, rattles and other ceremonial paraphernalia, much of it made before or shortly after white contact, when the culture was still intact. Over the years, the museum has exercised a rare institutional generosity by lending objects from its collection for native use and encouraging new work by young artists.

On a brief visit to the museum, I found that the carving shed, which was built in the vertical hewn-plank and gable-roofed style of the traditional native longhouse, was still in operation. Henry Hunt died in 1985, but a young Vancouver Island carver named Tim Paul was at work on a 26-ft. yellow cedar totem pole for Canada's new National Museum of Man in Ottawa. Paul has worked at the museum for 15 years, most of that time with Henry Hunt's son, Richard, who succeeded his father as chief carver. (The elder Hunt developed his craft under the legendary Mungo Martin, who came to the museum in the early 1950s.)

The new pole will be the first Paul has completed entirely on his own. He worked with Art Thompson on another, created in Vancouver's Stanley Park. Paul began by making exact reproductions of historic poles in the museum's collection, using calipers to ensure accuracy. Tentatively, he introduced more of himself in his carvings, afraid of offending his elders. Their reaction was encouraging. "It's emotionally rewarding when your people accept your work," Paul said. "You feel more alive as an artist when you do something of your own."

Indeed, it seems to me that any art that fails to grow will perish. But for a few twists of fate, Northwest Coast art and culture would have gone the way of the Incas and the Mayas, who suffered an even more violent decline. On a trip to the Queen Charlotte Islands in 1883, Port Townsend's James G. Swan called the area "an Indian's paradise," with "plenty of fish and berries in summer, wild geese and ducks in myriads in the fall and all winter, and with but little physical exertion their every want is supplied." Northwest natives reaped the benefits of agricultural life with none of its usual burdens. Thanks to this benevolent environment, they achieved an uncommon level of social, spiritual and artistic development.

Swan, who happened to be collecting artifacts for the Smithsonian, witnessed a culture in transition. Within a few years, the accumulated effects of disease, the Church and white justice decimated the native population in number and spirit. Sea captains counted floating corpses like so many boom logs; it is estimated that at least one-third of the total coastal population of 60,000 natives perished between 1835 and 1885. Of the eight distinct tribes that occupied the coast between Puget Sound and Alaska, only the Kwakiutl continued to practice the outlawed potlatch ceremony, and thus were able to develop their art in the ensuing decades. The potlatch is a ritual of song and dance and gift giving, in which carved masks and totems figure prominently; it is a cornerstone of the Northwest Coast tradition.

In what John McKillop called the "degenerative tourist period" that followed, the existing art was either chopped up for firewood, left to rot or spirited away to collections around the world. The 42-ft. dugout canoe sealed in a glass chamber outside the Provincial Museum is one of countless examples. Built in 1892 by a 70-year-old Nootka craftsman, "Weetatset" ("Going-to-War") was donated to the Province 40 years later in exchange for a Wee McGregor power saw. By and large, the curio craft that survived was smaller in scope, entirely derivative and commercial.

All that has changed in the last two decades. In his 1984 book, *The Legacy,* Peter Macnair, head of ethnology at the British Columbia Provincial Museum,

estimated no fewer than 200 serious Indian artists in the Province. Judging from the amount of work I saw throughout the Northwest, that number could be much higher today. On one weeknight in Seattle, I had to pry my way into a sold-out lecture by artist Barry Herem about new trends in Northwest Coast art. I didn't hear much from the hallway, but the message was clear. The art had long since transcended the reproduction of traditional forms. Herem showed slides of motorized transformation masks and 25-ft. wide thunderbirds. He described sculptures in every imaginable medium—plastic, fiberglass, bronze and steel. If Northwest furniture makers were reluctant to paint their work or use materials other than wood, the original Northwest woodworkers and their descendents felt no such constraints. Virtually every form of native woodwork is drenched in color, and many artists make dramatic use of abalone, copper, feathers and precious metals as well.

Artwork from the Northwest Coast is once again traveling the globe, albeit on much better terms this time around. Contemporary carvings can be found in museums and embassies from Africa to Japan and in homes and public places all over the Pacific Northwest.

In Herem's talk, and almost everywhere I went, the same four names kept cropping up: Bill Reid, Bill Holm, Robert Davidson and Duane Pasco. More than anyone, Reid is credited with having begun the process of reviving the art. Largely through his work in silver and gold, Reid began to

Inspired by a variety of Northwest Coast styles, Duane Pasco has been carving mask, totems and dugout canoes since the late 1950s.

explore the form in the 1950s and popularized it in his publications. The 69-year-old Reid, who is of Haida origin, worked closely with Bill Holm, the non-native Seattle scholar who deciphered the visual code in his now classic book, *Northwest Coast Art: An Analysis of Form.* Holm also taught many of the young crop of native and white artists and carvers. Davidson and Pasco are considered two of the most influential contemporary masters of Northwest Coast carving. I went to see Pasco first.

"I could smell the cedar and smell the smoke from the driftwood fire, the seaweed cooking," Pasco said, recalling the steaming of a bent-wood box 30 years before. With the making of that container, he had fallen in love with the simple logic of the craft—the elemental concept of splitting a board, cutting the kerfs and using hot rocks and water to bend it. The source for Pasco's box was the anthropologist Franz Boas, who was one of the first to document the Northwest Coast art in the 19th century. It took lots of tries to get it right, "but when you're done," Pasco said, "you have a beautiful container."

After a brief fling as a commercial artist, Pasco, who was raised in Alaska and Seattle, began carving what he now calls "quasi-Indian stuff" in the late 1950s. He became inspired by northern styles—Haida, Tlingit, Tsimshian—and learned to reproduce them, but Bill Holm's book put the work in a context he could understand. "Before Holm's analysis," Pasco is quoted as saying, "I could look right at 19th-century masks, boxes, bowls, totem poles...without seeing the unchanging, underlying forms in every piece. They're so highly developed, it took me many years to understand and use them."

"I don't think I have a style now," Pasco told me at his log home on Bainbridge Island, not far from the Seattle ferry. Pasco's wife, Katie, who is his business manager and frequent spokeswoman, explained that "the more he sees the old pieces, the less he's able to focus on their differences." Pasco described his current work as "pan-coastal." But there's a lot of himself in it, which he thinks may be more traditional than strict adherence to old forms. A client of Pasco's in New York calls his totem pole an "upright motif." "I don't worry about being

Detail of the carving on one of Duane Pasco's steamed and kerf-bent chests.

Photo by Duane Pasco

authentic anymore," Pasco said. "It just *is*. It's a lot more fun that way."

This raised the obvious question, the question everyone hated to answer, but the one they all knew was coming: How can a non-native work in such a culture-bound, traditional art form? Pasco's first response was from the hip. "I really don't regard it as an issue," he said.

But the issue wouldn't go away. In Seattle, I visited two shops that specialize in Northwest Coast art—The Legacy, owned by Mardonna Austin-McKillop (John McKillop's wife), and the new Bailey Nelson Gallery. At The Legacy, which was founded in 1933, McKillop told me that 99.9% of their work was made by native artists. Almost all of the carvings on display at the Bailey Nelson, on the other hand, were made by whites, many of them taught by Bill Holm. The problem, McKillop felt, was with the white artists who adopted the trappings of native culture and whose work feigned authenticity—the "wannabees," as one anthropologist called them. "It's great," she said, "when it's used as a jumping-off point. But it gets skewed in the public mind."

In Port Townsend, I had been particularly impressed by the work of two relatively unknown non-natives whose styles were clearly rooted in the Northwest Coast tradition. Linda Auernhammer took carving classes from both Pasco and Robert Davidson, among others, but her extraterrestrial masks, like the one above right, come from another world of her own making. "That's why I do contemporary stuff," Auernhammer told me. "I want to have more fun with it."

Likewise, Bob Cowgill hoped to avoid offending the natives whose work he had admired for 20 years. "You don't want to feel like you're ripping them off," he said. "They've been ripped off enough." But most of Cowgill's carved knife handles, spoons and sculptures are extremely traditional. The carvings often relate the story of some real or imagined experience. "I don't really copy their stuff," he said, "it just comes from the same source—animals, the environment." Cowgill rarely sells his work, preferring to give it away or trade it with friends.

"When the art is divorced from the culture," Pasco told me later, "it loses its reason for being." But that hasn't discouraged him from doing his art. To the contrary, he has immersed himself in his adoptive culture. Pasco explained that natives do art for two reasons: money and identity. Non-natives do it for money and love. "It becomes an obsession," Pasco added, "a whole hungry pursuit."

Even his critics acknowledge that Pasco has given a lot back. In the workshops he conducts up and down the coast and the almost two years he spent teaching at 'Ksan, a native craft community in British Columbia, Pasco has influenced a generation of native carvers. Before leaving, I visited a makeshift work site in a cemetery on the Klallam reservation, where Pasco was instructing and assisting local carvers in the construction of a two-man Salish canoe. Pasco knew as much about building it as anyone around. As he explained in an interview with the *Wall Street Journal* a few years ago, "The art is in the culture, not in an individual's genes."

According to people I spoke with on both sides of the border, the relationship between culture and art is viewed quite differently in Canada and the United States. To put it simply, Canadians are more preoccupied with the cultural context. This may reflect the involvement of museums and anthropologists in the preservation of the art, as well as Canada's multicultural orientation—the country is often called a "mosaic," never a "melting pot." It's

Photo by Robert Zinnedge

Linda Auernhammer is one of a number of non-natives whose contemporary carving is clearly inspired by traditional Northwest forms.

Robert Davidson, above, applies North-west Coast design in several media. Above right: This wooden killer-whale carving, about 8 in. in dia., is a model for a much larger bronze sculpture.

also true that Northwest Coast art flourished north of Puget Sound, where the Canadian government avoided the Indian wars that were endemic in the American Northwest. For whatever reasons, as Katie Pasco said, "Canadians who buy art, buy the ethnicity. People in the U.S. are buying sculpture."

People look to Robert Davidson for both. In his graphic art and carvings, Davidson is at once among the most innovative and traditional of contemporary Haida artists. Picking up the stitches of an unraveled culture, Davidson erected a totem pole in his home village of Massett in the Queen Charlotte Islands in 1969. It was the first to be raised in the Haida homeland in this century. In the tradition of the potlatch, the pole was Davidson's way of giving something back to the old people in his community, and perhaps validating his own claim to the culture at the same time. But its full significance did not become clear until the pole went up. "By releasing the old knowledge," Davidson has said, "you acquire it."

I visited Davidson's studio in British Columbia, within view of the Strait of

Georgia, the riverine passage between Vancouver Island and the mainland. Using a combination of European chisels and traditional crooked knives, Davidson and his apprentice, Larry Rosso, had several cedar masks in progress. Davidson explained that most of his masks receive a gently faceted, knife-textured finish because he "doesn't have the heart to sand." It's a painstaking process, but "it's that kind of finish," he said, "that gives you the charisma—it brings you right in."

"The art form didn't arrive on anybody's doorstep," Davidson said. "It was a process." He forged his own apprenticeship in the 1960s, by visiting museums and traveling door to door in search of old pieces to mine for ideas. "Ideas, if they work, become part of the culture," he said. "Cultural ideas discarded are life come to an end."

Davidson also worked with Bill Reid for two years and was greatly influenced by his grandfather, Robert Davidson, Sr., who was the last dugout-canoe builder in Massett. Davidson has yet to build a dugout, but his grandfather taught him to pay attention to the spirit of the creatures around him. "The art is meaningless," Davidson learned, "unless it goes with the ceremony." So I was not surprised that he felt "something missing" in a lot of non-native carving. It was as difficult an issue for him to resolve as for the whites whom I spoke with. "At first it really bothered me," he said, "but then I realized it was my own insecurity as an artist. Now it doesn't bother me. I'm just very intrigued by them."

Davidson's work is the closest thing to what Ivan Doig called "carved music." He participates in potlatches and other traditional events and even formed a dance group, which provides a context for many of his masks. "It's not so much to bring the art back in time, as to bring it forward," he explained. It's important to learn the vocabulary by imitating old forms, but Davidson felt it was time to move beyond what he calls "the anthropology stage." "Every medium has its boundaries," he said. Exploring them pushes Davidson and his art forward.

Davidson works in several media—wood, bronze and silkscreen. His masks, totem poles and sculptures have achieved the kind of recognition few woodworkers dare to imagine. The masks sell for $7,500 to $10,000—not the sort of thing you'd wear to a Halloween party, but then, as Davidson says, "they're not ordinary masks." (He told me he learned pricing from Bill Reid, who knows he hasn't charged enough if the customer is still standing.)

Two of Davidson's most spectacular projects are light-years from the Queen Charlotte Islands. He recently installed three totem poles in an atrium in downtown Toronto ("The Three Watchmen") and three in the Pepsico Sculpture Park, 25 miles north of New York City ("Three Variations on Killer Whale Myth"). In these sculptures, Davidson grapples with what may be the central theme of Northwest Coast art—transformation.

Native mythology is rich with accounts of fish and fowl transforming themselves into humans, and many natives claim a totemic bond with the wildlife around them. As Bill Holm and Bill Reid wrote in *Dialogue on Craftsmanship and Aesthetics*, "In Northwest Coast art…, they weren't bound by the silly feeling that it's impossible for two figures to occupy the same space at the same time." Davidson's carvings, like the poles at right, eloquently express this idea. In a new 20-ft. pole, to be entitled "Breaking the Totem Barrier," Davidson continues to transform himself.

In the end, transformation is at the heart of Northwest woodworking. Carpenters are now cabinetmakers; cabinetmakers have become furniture makers; furniture makers want to be artists; and everyone is learning about business. Whites are adopting native culture and imagery in their work, while natives are building a reputation as international artists. Many marriages that once nourished the early stages of these transitions have been jettisoned like a spent booster rocket. Everywhere, collaboration, once the exception, has become the rule. As Gary Pagenstecher put it, "There's a community of people. Even if we're not always working together, we know that they're there."

Even the so-called "Northwest style" of furniture I'd been seeking, if it ever existed, is comprised of a potpourri of influences—Krenov, Maloof, Nakashima, Arts and Crafts, Greene and Greene. While Northwest furniture is often characterized by dazzling woods, organic forms and conspicuous joinery, it may be more notable for what it generally lacks—color, materials other than wood and reverence for early American traditions.

Very few of the craftspeople I visited on my trip managed to negotiate all of these stylistic and economic convolutions without a few pratfalls. But I remember, in particular, the comments of one woodworker who had, to paraphrase Kurt Vonnegut, lost a few teeth in the clutchless shifts of life. Gary Rogowski of Portland told me: "It's changing too fast, they keep changing the rules." His Arts and Crafts portfolio of a few years ago is now passé. "I'm trying to make the edges sharper and the colors brighter," Rogowski said. "You can't just put an oil finish on something and expect it to hide. It's got to shout, it's got to grab your sleeve. I don't think talent, or even craftsmanship, is the issue anymore." Still, he added, "I'm making work that pleases me."

Not many craftspeople felt they'd arrived or were completely satisfied with the balance they'd struck between these polarities. Quite a few have given up trying. But most of those I met seemed to relish the struggle.

Scott Landis is a freelance writer and photographer. In addition to numerous magazine articles, he is the author of The Workbench Book, *published in 1987 by The Taunton Press.*

These red cedar totems, carved in 1986 by Davidson for the Pepsico Sculpture Park at Purchase, N. Y., deal with the mythology of transformation, a central theme in Northwest Coast art.

Index

Books and production staff

Editor: *Paul Bertorelli*
Editorial assistants: *Martha Gee, Cassandra Lincoln, Margaret Pendergast*
Designer: *Henry Roth*
Layout artists: *Cathy Cassidy, Steve Hunter, Marianne Markey*
Art assistants: *Jodie A. Delohery, Iliana Koehler, Cindy Nyitray*
Copy/production editor: *Ruth Dobsevage*
Typesetter: *Valerie Lutters*
Print production manager: *Peggy Dutton*

Magazine staff

Editor: *Dick Burrows*
Associate editor: *Sandor Nagyszalanczy*
Assistant editors: *Jim Boesel, Alan Platt, Charley Robinson*

Typeface: ITC Garamond Book
Paper: Warrenflo, 70 lb., neutral pH
Printer and binder: Ringier America, New Berlin, Wisconsin